**Tahar Ben Jelloun** was born in Fez, Morocco, and immigrated to France in 1961. A novelist, essayist, critic and poet, Ben Jelloun is an award-winning and internationally bestselling author. Among his many books are: *The Sand Child*, *Leaving Tangier*, *The Sacred Night* and *The Blinding Absence of Light*.

**Aneesa Abbas Higgins** is the translator of numerous works from the French. Among the authors she has translated are Nina Bouraoui, Ali Zamir and Elisa Shua Dusapin. Two of her translations have been winners of English PEN awards and her translation of *Seven Stones* by Vénus Khoury-Ghata was shortlisted for the Scott Moncrieff Prize.

**Jeremy Harding** is a contributing editor at the *London Review of Books*, where he has written often about the Maghreb and the Middle East. His books include *Border Vigils: Keeping Migrants out of the Rich World*, and *Mother Country*, a memoir. His translations of Arthur Rimbaud's poetry are published by Penguin.

# ON TERRORISM

Conversations with my daughter

## TAHAR BEN JELLOUN

### Translated by
Aneesa Abbas Higgins

### *With an Introduction by*
Jeremy Harding

**SMALL ✂ AXES**

HopeRoad Publishing
PO Box 55544
Exhibition Road
London SW7 2DB

www.hoperoadpublishing.com

First published as *Le terrorisme expliqué à nos enfants*
© Editions du Seuil 2016
Translation © Aneesa Abbas Higgins

This edition first published in 2020 by Small Axes,
an imprint of HopeRoad

Copyright © Tahar Ben Jelloun 2016

Introduction © Jeremy Harding

The right of Tahar Ben Jelloun to be identified as the author of this work has been asserted by him in accordance with the Copyright, Designs and Patents Act 1988.

All rights reserved. No part of this book may be reproduced, stored in a retrieval system or transmitted in any form or by any means, electronic, mechanical, photocopying, recording or otherwise, without the prior permission of the publisher.
This book is sold subject to the condition that it shall not, by way of trade or otherwise, be lent, re-sold, hired out or otherwise circulated without the publisher's prior consent in any form of binding or cover other than that in which it is published and without a similar condition including this condition being imposed on the subsequent purchaser.
A CIP catalogue record for this book is available from the British Library.

This book is supported by the Institut français (Royaume-Uni) as part of the Burgess programme.

ISBN 978-1-9164671-1-8
eISBN 978-1-9164671-6-3

Printed and bound by Clays Ltd, Elcograf S.p.A

# Introduction

In November 2015 more than 130 people died in and around Paris, in co-ordinated attacks carried out by roughly a dozen terrorists and their network of accomplices in the name of Islamic State (IS) or Daesh. The Bataclan, a rock music venue on the Boulevard Voltaire, was the site of the worst atrocities, with 90 dead and many more wounded. Paris had been hit earlier, on 7 January, by jihadists targeting the editors of the satirical weekly *Charlie Hebdo.* The murders at the magazine were followed by further violence and on 9 January four Jewish people were gunned down in a kosher supermarket. Altogether the attackers killed 17 victims, including three police officers, and wounded 22. There were other 'Islamist' incidents in France in 2015, including a murder by a delivery driver who strangled his employer in a truck and later severed his head. At the time, decapitation was a glamorous form of execution favoured by IS, just as it once was by the French. But the guillotine was used for the last time in 1977 and François Mitterrand abolished the death penalty in 1981.

Tahar Ben Jelloun's imagined conversations with his daughter, published here for the first time in English, appeared in France in 2016, as the country took stock of the previous year's horrors. By then Ben Jelloun and his family were mourning another loss - that of their relative, French-Moroccan photographer Leila Alaoui, who died in January after an attack on a restaurant in Burkina Faso, claimed by two jihadist groups operating in Africa. Six months later 86 people were murdered by a terrorist who drove a truck into the crowds celebrating Bastille Day in Nice. The attack was claimed by IS.

It's hardly surprising that one of the topics between father and daughter in this lucid book is fear: not just fear for one's life - of 'something awful lurking', as his daughter suggests - but a generic fear of Islam and 'Muslims'. More than once she asks her father whether it makes sense to be 'afraid of Islam' - a religion espoused in practice, or in name, by nearly a quarter of the world's population, including the two people having this discussion. It's a demoralising possibility, and one that's never far away in France, where the events of 2015 were not the first of their kind. In the 1980s a wave of bombings masterminded by a Shia Islamist with links to Hezbollah left more than a dozen people dead and hundreds wounded. The numbers rose in the 1990s, with attacks by the Groupe Islamiste Armé, based in Algeria, and again - dramatically - after IS proclaimed its caliphate: more than 240 people died in France at the hands of violent Islamists between 2014 and 2020.

But fears about Islam are also rampant in the US, since the 9/11 attacks (nearly 3000 dead), and in Britain, where Islamist suicide bombers killed 52 people and wounded hundreds more in 2005. In 2013 Lee Rigby, a British soldier, was murdered by Islamic extremists near his barracks in Woolwich. In 2017 Salman Abedi blew himself up in the Manchester Arena, taking 22 lives as well as his own and wounding more than 800 others. In 2019 Usman Khan, a convicted terrorist released from prison on licence, stabbed three people to death at an offender rehabilitation conference in London: he was a follower of the UK jihadist-Salafist network Al Mahajiroun.

Ben Jelloun and his daughter are right to worry that Muslims are now seen in the West as dangerous others, staking out the free world, lying low and preparing to strike when it suits them. But these fears have their counterpart in Muslim communities, recoiling from the fury of the West. The interrogation centres in Algeria during its war of independence are still a difficult subject in France, as is the legacy of colonialism in general. Muslims all over the world shudder at the mention of American torture chambers in Abu Ghraib, the bombing of Baghdad in 2003 and the assaults on Fallujah the following year. Generations of stigmatised migrants and new, would-be immigrants have first-hand experience of racism in host cultures, including attempts by the American executive to bar Muslims from entering the US in 2017.

'Does the state have the right to defend itself,' Ben Jelloun's daughter asks him, 'by responding to terror with more terror?'

It's one of the most startling questions in the book. Another, just as powerful, is whether we should give free rein to our fears, even when they have a basis in fact. Should we - do we - inflate them into generic fantasies about 'Muslims'? What exactly is the terror in our heads? Why does a Western 'we' imagine a hostile 'them' in such over-inflated numbers, flourishing abroad and lurking at home? It's true that thousands of IS recruits were born and bred in Europe, but even at the height of its *folie des grandeurs* the Daesh caliphate had nothing comparable to the personnel and firepower deployed in the Middle East by the US-led coalition in the early 2000s, or later by Russia and Syria. Putin and the warrior democracies of the global north have filled the Middle East with death and oppression and struck fear in people's hearts, whether they put their faith in the Western model or reviled it.

As we try to wrestle fact from fiction, it helps to bear in mind that violent Islamists have inflicted vastly higher casualties on Muslims than non-Muslims in the last thirty years or so, as Ben Jelloun reminds his daughter. Vengeful military campaigns, like the West's destruction of Iraq, add to the Muslim death toll and reinforce the asymmetry of this reckless face-off. So does state persecution of Rohingya people in Burma and Uighurs in China, or India's citizenship act of 2019, which discriminates against Muslim non-nationals. All such policies increase the likelihood of terrorism and pop-up caliphates.

But how is Ben Jelloun to unpack a mass of complicated truths and half-truths for his daughter? The young are as smart as their elders and she is no exception. However, this is an imaginary conversation: she is the medium enabling the father - now in his seventies - to test his own positions for himself. He discovers that he is flatly opposed to terrorism as a force for change or a weapon of grievance. Interestingly, he suspects that jihadism in France and other Western countries draws on a long nihilist tradition (which comes with a death wish as part of the thinking): he shares this idea with the French political scientist Olivier Roy, who sees European jihadism less as a 'radicalisation of Islam' than an 'Islamisation of radicalism'.*

Ben Jelloun, a Moroccan writer who moved to France more than forty years ago, has fully absorbed the French secular republican tradition. 'The application of the principle of secularity,' he writes here, 'is a mark of civilisation.' And so, when the conversation turns to freedom of expression, he defends the right to print offensive cartoons mocking Islam (and the Prophet), as *Charlie Hebdo* did before the fatal attack in 2015. He doesn't raise the possibility that the cartoons might

---

\* *Jihad and Death: The Global Appeal of Islamic State* by Olivier Roy, translated by Cynthia Schoch, Hurst, 2017.

have been a greater taunt to France's Muslim minority - already the object of discrimination, and occasionally contempt - than they were to prestigious brokers of Islam around the world. At the same time he disapproves of their publication. He is eloquent in defence of Islam as a religion of peace and tolerance: a religion with many strands, open to many readings, betrayed in his view, and the view of millions of fellow Muslims, by the new jihadism and the rise of a fastidious, doctrinaire interpretation, with its origins in Saudi Arabia, disseminated on the back of Saudi oil revenues.

But he is just as harsh on atrocities committed in the name of Judaism and Christianity, and critical of France's failure to provide decent housing, education and equal opportunities for generations of immigrants and their children. Surveying the international scene, he is alarmed by Western foreign policy in the Middle East, now and in the past. He has a strong sense of colonial injustice, and even though he passes far too quickly over Morocco's annexation of the Western Sahara, he has always supported the Palestinians. He believes they are justified in resisting colonial settlement in the occupied territories, and the Israeli blockade of Gaza. But there are tougher issues here, raised by his daughter. What distinguishes 'resistance' from 'terrorism'? Is it a matter of methods or does it come down to the justice of a particular cause? Ben Jelloun does his best to keep a clear distinction between reason and unreason, resistance and terror, throughout this discussion. It's a hard task, as historians of the resistance to Vichy and the Nazi occupation in France could tell us, and he hesitates over the aggressive militancy of Hamas in the face of a desperate situation.

But the point of these imagined conversations is that they're free-running, open-hearted and fluent: Aneesa Abbas Higgins's translation catches the tone perfectly. Bold ideas, asserted early on, are revised or reconsidered further down the line. As the father's thoughts unfold, his daughter nudges them this way and that with questions which sound more innocent than they really are. The result is a plea for enlightenment and education: above all in the teaching of religion and difference, where France has a poorer record than the UK. 'We'll do everything in our power to make sure a new generation of young people emerges, young people who won't be duped into swallowing any old lies,' Ben Jelloun announces. But the ball is in his daughter's court. Hers is the generation that will need to forage on its own to work around the shortcomings of formal education - and they'll have a duty to keep their parents up to speed.

*Jeremy Harding*
*Bordeaux, January 2020*

# How to Talk to our Children about Terrorism

We must tell our children the truth. We should never underestimate their capacity to absorb distressing information, to confront the awful nature of reality. Children are no tougher or better equipped than adults to deal with such things, but they are receptive to them. If we choose our words carefully, strike the appropriate tone and find the right moment, we can ask our children to process the truth without fear of disastrous consequences to their development. Lies and denials can lead to problems and give rise to deep-rooted fears. And children aren't easily fooled; they glean information from sources adults know nothing about. If we sugar-coat the truth and lie about harsh realities, if we deny the facts or wrap them in cotton wool, we run the risk of cutting our children off from the reality of life, in all its beauty and violence. And in the end, they'll know they're being lied to and insist on being told the truth.

Fairy tales are full of cruelty. Little Red Riding Hood, Bluebeard, Aladdin and other *Tales of the Thousand and One Nights* are terrifying; no doubt this is why we like them so much and why their appeal is both timeless and universal. At their most basic level, fairy tales tell of the struggle between good and evil, a battle that children understand only too well, in all its complexity.

However many precautions parents take these days to protect their children from violence, they cannot shield them completely from the brutality of some of today's video games and music videos. The film industry, too, plays its part in perpetuating the vision of a world in which chainsaw massacres are everyday events. And then of course there is pornography, a mere click away as soon as parents turn their backs.

Families that lost a loved one in the *Charlie Hebdo* and Bataclan attacks of January and November 2015 suffered terrible trauma, adults as well as children. All of them are in need of solace and clear explanations. It takes patience and skilful guidance to help people accept the reality of unprecedented, intolerable events. But first, people need time for the painful realities of grieving. Loss and absence leave gaping holes in our lives, whatever our age or gender, and children, probably more than adults, need precise, well-chosen words if they are to understand.

Understanding is the beginning of acceptance. Acceptance does not mean excusing or forgetting; to accept is to reject the illusion that the past can be changed. Acceptance means learning to look reality in the face and understand that life is not a pretty picnic where everything is wonderful and everyone is kind, friendly, generous and helpful. It means acknowledging that evil exists and that anyone is capable of doing harm, whether it be for pleasure or financial gain. People harbouring an inner 'thirst for evil' don't wear it stamped on their forehead. It all goes on inside their head, where no one can penetrate, not even their parents, who are often the first to be surprised by the appalling acts committed by their son or daughter.

What follows is a semi-imagined dialogue between one of my daughters and me; naturally there are some questions that will be of more interest to girls. One does not always talk to boys and girls in the same way.

To explain is of course neither to justify nor to excuse; it is simply a way of enabling those who wonder what is going on to come to a greater understanding.

# The other day …

'Dad, I'm terrified.'

'What do you mean?'

'I'm scared. I'm scared all the time.'

'Why? Your family are here, your friends are here. You have everything you want. So, why this fear?'

'Because I know there's something awful lurking, but I don't know what it is. Sometimes I see horrible, scary images. All dark and blurry.'

'Are you thinking about the people who were killed in the Bataclan?'

'Yes, but it's not just that. I keep thinking I could have been one of those people at the Bataclan, me or my friends. It's like I'm going to die, and I'm scared, but it doesn't happen.'

'Can you tell me what it actually feels like, this fear?'

'It's like a great, heavy weight, coming towards us. It dwarfs us. Or else something happens in the back of my throat. I can't get my words out; I can't breathe. I'm out of my depth. It's lots of different things, really. But mostly, it's like a weight, yes, that's it, a weight on my chest, and I can't work out where it comes from.'

'What you're describing is terror. A feeling of dread. Sometimes it makes you panic. You feel unhinged; you're defenceless and vulnerable. It makes you weak. You can't think straight, your brain's all scrambled. You think there's something horrible and violent just around the corner, but you don't know which direction it's coming from, and you feel helpless. People use terror as a weapon, people who want to force their ideas on the rest of us. They use it to undermine our way of life, our way of thinking. It's the best weapon they can find. They don't care about the law and people's rights, they're bent on death and destruction. Most of us accept that people with different ideas can live together peacefully. We have arguments and discussions about things we don't agree on – we don't have to actually come to blows. It's what we call civil society. We have an unwritten agreement we call the social contract. But terrorists have turned their backs on all that. They're not interested in reasonable discussion. They don't want to live by our social contract. They've put themselves outside civil society.'

'Is that the same as a civilised society?'

'Yes, it is. And the social contract is a way for us all to get along well with each other. What it boils down to is quite simple: I respect your rights and you respect mine. It's an agreement based on values we all share, values that make us human and distinguish us from animals. As I explained in my book on racism, we're all different and we're all the same. If we want to live together in peace, we have to respect the laws and rights that go with being a citizen – the words "citizen" and "civilised" both come from the same Latin word, *civis*. A civilised person is simply a citizen who lives by the laws of society, who accepts the rules and regulations laid down over a long period of time. It's a code we inherit from the generations that came before us. A code with hundreds of laws. In France, we have an enormous book called the Napoleonic Code full of all those rules and regulations.'

'So civilisation means finding a way of living together?'

'That's right. But there's more to it than that. Being civilised has been described as having "an inherited set of beliefs, customs and knowledge" that we use to guide us in everything we do. That was how one author (Antoine de Saint-Exupéry, who wrote *The Little Prince)* put it. Another writer, Thomas Mann, said that being civilised means having a blend of "good sense, wisdom, kindness, decency, doubt, open-mindedness and quick-thinking". Being civilised means making progress, making improvements; it means having kindness and respect for other people as your goal. It has nothing to do with being educated. Someone like your granny, who's never been to school, can be perfectly civilised. We pass on our values in the way we live our lives. Our minds are far more important than money and material things.'

'And if we stop being civilised?'

'You're left with nothing but brute force and mindless violence. Killing and slaughtering. Once you stop accepting the law and start killing and massacring innocent people, you've become a terrorist. You're not respecting human life. You've broken the social contract. Remember, the social contract isn't written down anywhere, but we understand what it is. We know from experience that it's wrong to steal and rape and kill. The social contract helps us to be decent human beings, worthy of respect. Without it, there's nothing but the law of the jungle: might is right. No culture, no morality, no humanity.'

'And that's terrorism.'

'Exactly. Terrorism involves blackmail, too. Terrorists sometimes make threats before they carry out an atrocity.'

'What do you mean?'

'Well, for example, they send a message to the government saying: "If you don't do what we tell you, if you don't give in to our demands, we'll put a bomb in a crowded public place." They're taking the whole population hostage, if you like.'

'Yes, I know. I've seen films where that happens.'

'They make threats and spread fear. The message is: there's violence to come, people will be killed. And then everyone is seized by fear. Even the most powerful governments have no weapons against fear. The government has to reassure people but that's a difficult thing to do. After the Bataclan attacks the French government declared a prolonged state of emergency, which meant that the police could search people's homes without a warrant. But if a terrorist is determined to carry out an atrocity, there's not much you can do to stop them.'

'So, give me a definition of terrorism, then.'

'Well, to start with, terrorism is a means to an end, it's a *modus operandi*, a way of doing things. It's not a philosophy or a way of thinking. Terrorism means using violence against people or property to try and force a government to satisfy certain demands. And we don't usually know the identities of the people who make these demands, we don't know what they look like. Sometimes they just kill people at random. There's no particular goal or demand. The aim is simply to spread fear, so that everyone will say: "That could have been me." No one feels safe. It forces people to change the way they live; people stop going out in the evening, or they avoid public places because they're often chosen as targets. Life is seriously disrupted.'

'Do terrorists do it for money?'

'Some do. Or they might have a political or a religious goal. Or they might simply want to destabilise a country for reasons the public know nothing about.'

'That's how my cousin Leila Alaoui was killed in Burkina Faso! She was having a quiet dinner in an Italian restaurant in Ougadougou and she died, along with twenty-nine other people. It was horrible.'

'Yes, Leila was in the wrong place at the wrong time. How was she to know that Ouagadougou was going to be attacked by terrorists? She had no idea.'

'Were they jihadists?'

'They were people on a mission to kill and spread terror. What for? Why did they murder all those people in such a spectacular way? Maybe it was to tell us that their way of seeing the world is the only right way.'

'And what about people who say they're acting in the name of jihad?'

'People who say they are waging jihad are harking back to an old tradition. But we'll talk more later about what jihad has come to mean these days.'

'Okay, I'll ask you about jihad later. Let's get back to terror.'

'Using terror as a means to an end goes back a long way, starting with the French Revolution in 1789. The period from September 1793 to July 1794 is known as the Reign of Terror. The Revolutionary Government decided to wage a vicious and brutal campaign against people they considered to be enemies of the Revolution. Eventually they set up a dictatorship and began executing more and more people, including Marie Antoinette, the queen. They forgot about law and justice and ruled by terror. No one was safe; anyone suspected of being an enemy was arrested and rapidly put to death. Everyone was afraid. There have been other regimes that used terror like this throughout the nineteenth and twentieth centuries, for example in certain South American and African countries. At the end of the nineteenth century, a Russian named Mikhail Bakunin devised the doctrine of anarchism, a doctrine that rejected all laws and refused to obey any authority. Its slogan was "no gods, no masters". There were anarchists, inspired by this doctrine, who killed people, usually members of the upper classes. So that gives you two different historical examples of terror being used for political means. The anarchists didn't kill in the name of God, like jihadists do now. And you could be an anarchist without necessarily becoming a terrorist. But the people who become jihadists these days are intent on waging war in the name of Islam. Their aim is to kill and die.

'There was a period at the end of the nineteenth century in France when there was a great deal of anarchist activity. One of the better known anarchists was a man known by the name Ravachol (1859–92), who was condemned to death and guillotined for the crimes he committed in the name of anarchism.'

'What exactly is anarchism?'

'It means there's no hierarchy. No one is more important than anyone else; there are no masters, no bosses, no state, no government, no police force, no order. It means a permanent struggle against any kind of order, whether it be social, religious or political. Everything is called into question, all the existing structures are destroyed.'

'But why did anarchists kill people?'

'To spread panic and disorder. Basically the anarchists wanted to do away with the state and with all private property. In their eyes, humanity would have been better off without those things.'

'But that's chaos!'

'Yes it is. Nothing is safe. Nobody's property is any safer than anyone else's.'

'Is such a thing possible? A society where there's no private ownership?'

'No, it's just an illusion.'

'What do you mean?'

'It's an ideal. The anarchists in France and Spain rejected the whole idea of private property. They attacked and killed people who owned property. But people have always wanted to own things, and it's the state's responsibility to protect property rights. The anarchists were a threat to security and so the state defended itself in any way it could. Most of the time its actions were within the law.'

'Does the state have the right to defend itself by responding to terror with more terror?'

'No, but in 1990, after a wave of terrorist attacks in Paris, the French interior minister made a declaration that became famous: "We shall terrorise the terrorists." In other words, use their methods to combat them. But the state is bound to respect the rule of law and follow it to the letter. Terrorists want the state to act illegally, to force it to defend itself by using methods that are outside the law and don't respect individual rights. As I said before, we need rules and regulations so that we can all live peacefully together. We need a body of law. If we don't respect that law, if we all do as we please and act only out of self-interest, for selfish reasons, it becomes impossible for us to live together.

Instead of the rule of law, there's only survival of the fittest, the law of the jungle.'

'Can you explain what you mean by the rule of law?'

'It means that the state acts in accordance with the principles and democratic values that aim to protect individuals. It's bound by laws and rules that it's not allowed to break, divert or distort. It means the state can't respond to terrorism with the blind, arbitrary violence that terrorists use. There can't be two forms of justice, one for peaceable citizens and another for those who take up arms in order to commit crimes against the innocent. The rule of law means the same justice for all, the same basic set of principles. Any individual arrested is presumed innocent until the courts have determined his or her guilt, or innocence. The rule of law is fundamental to any democracy. Corruption, favouritism, special favours and nepotism of any sort are all excluded, on principle.'

'What's nepotism?'

'Handing out jobs to members of your own family, not giving a chance to anyone else. It happens all over the world, but in Europe, any politician that does it can expect to be savaged by the press.'

'So what can democracy do against terrorism?'

'Well, as you've noticed, democracies aren't really prepared to cope with it. The only thing a democratic state can legitimately do is apply justice according to the law. The state should never resort to the practices used by terrorists. The battle has to be fought on several fronts using techniques such as intelligence-gathering, careful monitoring, being vigilant; in other words, working to prevent terrorist outrages. And all of this can be done quite legally by the state.'

'So why did France declare a state of emergency in November 2015?'

'The circumstances were exceptional. The last time France declared a state of emergency was in 1955, during the Algerian War. Then, it was in response to terrorist attacks by militants in the struggle for Algerian independence. Algeria was considered to be part of France in those days.'

'You mean politics and terrorism are closely linked?'

'Terrorism is a means of action, it's not an idea; it's the use of terror for political, religious or ideological ends. And sometimes it's a way of stealing, by demanding a ransom for a hostage. Or it could be for drug-trafficking or sex-slavery.

'During the January 2015 attacks in Paris, people were taken hostage at a kosher supermarket in Vincennes by Amedy Coulibaly, who was a friend of Said and Chérif Kouachi, the gunmen in the *Charlie Hebdo* attacks,. During the attack, Coulibaly made remarks that were both racist and religious. He chose that supermarket for a reason; he wanted to kill Jews. And three years earlier, on 19 March 2012, the terrorist Mohammed Merah targeted a Jewish school in Toulouse and killed three Jewish schoolchildren in cold blood. Then on 24 May 2014, Mehdi

Nemmouche attacked the Belgian Jewish Museum in Brussels and killed four people.

'Back in 1982, there was a terrorist attack against Jews in Paris on Rue des Rosiers that left six dead and twenty-two injured. The attack was carried out by Abou Nidal, a Palestinian Liberation Organisation (PLO) dissident turned professional killer. People say he was acting on the orders of Syrian president Hafez al-Assad, father of Bashar al-Assad, the current president of Syria, the one who is butchering the Syrian people. Hafez al-Assad wanted to punish France for giving aid to Lebanon, where there was a civil war raging at the time. And then later, in 1995, there was a terrorist attack at the rapid-transit RER station of Saint-Michel in Paris, carried out by a commando from the Algerian Islamist group GIA: eight people were killed and 117 injured. Algeria was in the midst of a civil war at the time, with Islamists on one side and the armed forces on the other. In 1991, Islamists had won the elections in Algeria but the authorities acted illegally and declared the results invalid. Islamists responded by declaring war on the Algerian government. The civil war went on for fifteen years and left more than 200,000 dead.'

'So, with terrorism, anything can happen?'

'Yes, anything. Terrorists murder indiscriminately. They use violence to advance a political cause, or else to extort money or gain other advantages.'

'So, when people take hostages and demand that the state change its policies, that's terrorism?'

'Yes, hostage-takers like that are terrorists, too. They're putting pressure on the state for political reasons, terrorising the civilian population in order to influence government policy.'

'Most of the time, terrorism is strictly political then, isn't it?'

'Yes, it is. Sometimes these groups commit random crimes, without necessarily giving any reasons. What they want is to instil panic in the civilian population, to stop people living their lives in a normal fashion. A bomb can explode anywhere. A killer can start shooting people he doesn't know, people who've done nothing to harm him. When a killer fires into a crowd and murders innocent people, anyone could become a target. And so, everyone takes fright.'

'Okay, so terrorism means spreading terror, I get that.'

'Yes, and what makes it so terrifying is that it's unpredictable: you can't see it, you don't know where or when it will strike. That's exactly what happened in Paris on 13 November 2015, when terrorists attacked the Bataclan and the cafés and restaurants in the neighbourhood around it. No one had ever imagined that a rock concert could be the scene of such an outrage, or that an evening spent having a drink with friends in a café could end in a massacre. It was an attack on people's way of life; on civilised, diverse individuals who live together in spite of their differences. And when terrorists attacked *Charlie Hebdo* in January 2015, that was an attack on freedom of expression, the freedom to write, think and draw. In other words, it was an attack on freedom itself.'

'So we're at its mercy because we don't know where it's coming from or where it's going to strike. Which explains the fear I was asking you about.'

'Yes, it's only natural to be afraid. The will to survive is a basic human instinct. But we have to overcome our fears! We must all do the best we can, especially the people who are in power. It's no good being guided by your emotions if you're responsible for making decisions and deciding on a course of action in moments of tragedy.'

'So what should be done?'

'There are some measures that have to be taken right away, something that governments are generally very good at doing. But we need to think long-term. Dealing swiftly with troublemakers at home is essential but France needs to rethink its relationship with certain countries in the Middle East, too. It needs to reconsider some of its policies towards those nations – and the same is true for other countries that are victims of Islamist terrorism. France declared a state of emergency and voted to prolong it.[1] This means that the state has given itself

---

1 The state of emergency was ended on 1 November 2017 and replaced by a new counter-terrorism law. The new law transposes some of the measures contained in the state of emergency rule into law. Human rights activists are concerned about the breaches of the rights of Muslims contained in the new law.

the right to legally investigate and search a suspect's premises without a search warrant if the police consider it necessary. People feel reassured by this. But as I said before, the state must act within the law. It can't use the same methods as the terrorists. Its first responsibility is to prevent further attacks; it has to act on intelligence and in consultation with other countries subjected to the same scourge. We have to go back to the origins of terrorism, research the causes of terrorism, however remote they are. We need to find out where it comes from and why people resort to such means to deliver their message to the nation and the government.'

'So the state of emergency is not enough?'

'No, it's not enough. It's just a quick fix. And when you consider that a section of the French population sees all Muslims, all Arabs, as potential jihadists, you can see the dangers. The police have sometimes gone too far, especially when carrying out searches in the *banlieues*, the immigrant suburbs. Human rights advocates have denounced what they consider to be "abuses under the state of emergency" and called on France not to prolong the state of emergency. The international body Human Rights Watch published a report in February 2016 that reads as follows: "The government has said it will ask parliament to renew the state of emergency for another three months. But it has not provided compelling evidence that would justify the need to continue these sweeping measures.

"'Absent such evidence, parliament should not renew the state of emergency," Human Rights Watch said.

"'Measures such as raids and searches should always require judicial authorization, which for urgent cases could take place under an accelerated procedure. The government also should ensure that people have prompt access to remedies for any damage caused by police action during any renewed state of emergency, and should carry out meaningful outreach about these remedies to targeted communities.""[2]

'Yes, I can see that everyone suffers, Muslims included. But Islamists aren't the only terrorists, are they? Can we talk some more about the history and origins of terrorism?'

'We've already talked a bit about the anarchists and their tactic of killing members of the establishment to undermine the state, the rule of law, the police and the army. The anarchists spread terror in Italy and Spain, as well as in France, and for a while between 1919 and 1923 Barcelona became the centre of anarchist-inspired terrorism carried out by militant trade unionists hostile to the army and the police. They organised boycotts and sabotage and waged a campaign of terror that killed as many as 30 civilians on a daily basis. Like the jihadists of today, the anarchists called on their followers to kill innocent

---

[2] https://www.hrw.org/news/2016/02/03/france-abuses-under-state-emergency

people at random, and to be ready to die themselves; their rallying cry was *"Viva la muerte!"* ("Long live death!") This particular wave of terror came to an end in 1923 when Primo de Rivera came to power in a coup d'état and established a brutal dictatorship over the whole of Spain. Like today's jihadists, the anarchists resorted to terror as a way of imposing their ideas on others. They placed themselves outside the law, and distanced themselves from the social contract. And when the French jihadists of today kill without warning, they're doing the same thing. They're ripping up the social contract, a point they've demonstrated by filming themselves burning their passports and broadcasting their videos. It's a way of defying their country.'

'What about the Norwegian man who killed so many people. Why did he do it? Was it for religious reasons?'

'You mean Anders Behring Breivik, the man who killed seventy-seven and injured 151 people on 22 July 2011. He acted entirely on his own, and we still don't fully understand why. He's been sentenced to life imprisonment. That was an example of an attack carried out by someone the police and intelligence services knew nothing about. Another example would be when members of a Japanese sect released sarin in the Tokyo metro on 20 March 1995. Sarin is a deadly poisonous gas and they killed twelve people and injured 5,500 with it. Attacks of this nature are more or less impossible to predict. It's happened in

Morocco, too; a bomb was planted in a crowded café, the *Argana*, in the famous Jemaa el-Fnaa square on 28 April 2011 by a man named Adil Othmani. He constructed the bomb and killed seventeen people that day, and injured a further twenty.'

'How does anyone get to be crazy enough to go out and kill people they don't know for reasons no one understands?'

'Some say it's what is known as nihilism, a negative way of seeing the world. Nihilists believe that everything is absurd, they reject life itself. They don't use reason or logic, and there's no attempt to search for good. Quite the opposite. They are dominated by what I see as a need to destroy: evil for evil's sake, with no attempt at justification. Or else it's a death wish they follow to its logical conclusion. But jihadists aren't nihilists; they're not driven by despair at the absurdity of existence. They're not mad, either. They do what they do in order to achieve their goal: to establish their ideal of a "pure Islamic State", where the only ruler is divine power.'

'So it's a battle between good and evil?'

'It's a bit more complicated than that. People sometimes say that terrorism is the weapon of the weak; for example, of people who are oppressed and desperate to free their country from an occupying power. Terrorist methods are often used by resistance movements. But acts of resistance are not at all the same as terrorist outrages. Morally, there's absolutely no comparison between resistance movements and terrorist groups. Violent terrorists with murky, unsavoury objectives have nothing in common with national liberation movements or resistance groups. Resistance is as honourable as terrorism is base and cowardly.'

'Would you say that resistance is a sort of terrorism-lite?'

'Absolutely not! The two should never be confused. Yes, there have been times in history when men and women have had no choice but to resort to violence in order to make their voices heard in a way that's certainly not legal. But it's human nature to revolt against slavery, against being deprived of your liberty and dignity. And that revolt might involve radical action. The word resistance comes from the Latin word *resistere,* which means to stand up against obstacles. Terrorism on the other hand comes from the Latin word *terrere*, which means to cause trembling. So remember: resistance should never be confused with terrorism. Terrorism is a means to an end, a course of action, it's not an idea or a philosophy. Resistance movements are often driven to use violent means in order to ensure that values such as dignity, justice and law can prevail. Terrorism couldn't care less about values. It can take many forms, but its aim is always death and destruction, even though the killers may have what they call an "ideal" behind their actions. The Resistance was very active in France during the Nazi occupation, planting bombs, for example, in the paths of Nazi officials.

But they didn't attack the civilian population; they targeted enemy soldiers and those who collaborated with them. And people did collaborate, including the French government of the time. People had a choice: resist or accept the humiliation of occupation. Some chose not only to accept but also to collaborate. The Resistance was considered by Nazi Germany and their French collaborators to be a terrorist organisation, but history now sees them purely as resistance fighters, in other words as men and women who fought in the name of civilisation and their own dignity. And remember that throughout history, resistance movements have always been labelled as terrorist by the authorities they were fighting against.'

'Careful, you're making excuses for terrorism! So you're saying there's good terrorism and bad terrorism?'

'Explaining something isn't the same as justifying it. History shows us that there have always been borderline cases in which resorting to terror was a necessary evil. Passive resistance and non-violence are nobly inspired, but they aren't always effective. I'll give you a few examples.

'In Ireland, armed struggle against the British went on for decades. And in Palestine, the Jewish people resorted to terrorism during the British Mandate. On 22 July 1946 the Zionist group the Irgun planted a bomb in the King David Hotel in Jerusalem, killing ninety-one people. And on 12 December 1947 at the Damascus Gate in the Old City of Jerusalem, they exploded a car bomb, killing twenty civilians. On 17 September 1948 the UN peace mediator, Count Bernadotte, was assassinated by a group known as the Stern Gang. All these terrorist attacks played a part in the creation of the State of Israel. They continued right up until the time the British left. And later, when Israel occupied parts of Palestine in June 1967, it was the Palestinians' turn to use the very same methods in their struggle to liberate their territory. The Algerians, too, had to fight for their independence; anyone who took up arms against the French was considered by the French government to be a terrorist. François Mitterrand, who was interior minister at the time, said: "Algeria is part of France." Mitterrand was one of those who signed the document calling for the Algerian "rebels" to be executed.

'Yes, he gave the order to execute Algerian people fighting to liberate their own country. The Algerian War of Independence went on from 1954 to 1962 and it's estimated (according to historian Sylvie Thénault) that 198 political prisoners were put to death during that time. One of them was a Frenchman by the name of Fernand Iveton. It tells you something about François Mitterrand that he signed that document, when there were other ministers who refused to sign it, people like Pierre Mendès France, who was president of the Council of Ministers back then. To be fair, though, when Mitterrand became president in 1981, he did approve the justice minister Robert Badinter's bill to make the death penalty illegal in France.'

'Yes, but that all happened during a war. And France isn't at war any more, is it?'

'Officially, no, we're not at war. But France is involved in countries where terrorism is a threat to French people's lives. There are more than 10,000 French soldiers deployed in several African states. Troops have been sent to Mali, the Central African Republic, Ivory Coast, Chad, Djibouti and Burkina Faso in response to calls for help. And France has been involved for some time now in the coalition of countries bombing bases of the so-called "Islamic State" in western Iraq and eastern Syria. So, in a way, France is at war, although this is certainly a new kind of war. And if you think about it, when terrorists targeted the hotel and the Italian restaurant in Ougadougou on 17 January 2016 and killed our beloved Leila Alaoui, it was France and French policies the terrorists were attacking. They killed 130 people that day. And when sixteen people (including four who were French) were killed in a terrorist attack on the beach at Grand-Bassam near the capital of Ivory Coast on 13 March 2016, it was France the terrorists were attacking.'

'So France isn't actually at war at the moment; it's just worried and scared. Okay. So now I'm going to ask you a tricky question. What about the Palestinian fighters? Are they terrorists, too?'

'As far as the State of Israel is concerned, yes they are. In the eyes of an established state like the State of Israel, anyone engaging in armed struggle against the occupation and colonisation of certain territories is a terrorist. A terrorist whose one intention, in this case, is to kill Jews. You can understand the logic of Israel's position: they are entitled to defend the territories they annexed and occupied after their victory in the Six-Day War in June 1967. When you look at it like this, their policy towards Palestinian fighters makes sense. And, don't forget that in 1991, Syria and Israel both accused each other of being "terrorist states". Let's just say that instead of agreeing to negotiate and live in peace, the stronger state often practises what is sometimes known as the politics of *fait accompli*. Once land has been annexed and occupied, anyone fighting to win back that land is considered to be a terrorist.'

'But why is that?'

'The State of Israel doesn't recognise Palestine. When the Palestinians drew up their charter, some of them wanted to include the destruction of the State of Israel as a goal, while others objected to this and agreed to negotiate with Israel. But negotiation has achieved nothing concrete for the Palestinian people. The State of Israel doesn't accept the legitimacy of the Palestinian struggle. In Israel's eyes, all Palestinians fighting to regain territories occupied by Israel are terrorists. There's also the fact that in the 1970s, as part of their campaign to have their rights recognised, some Palestinians did resort to violence and began hijacking planes and taking people hostage. They did it, as one Palestinian official said, in order to "bring the question of Palestine into the open and set it out before Western public opinion".'

'What exactly did they do?'

'In addition to hijacking planes, they attacked the Israeli Olympic team at the Munich Olympic Games in 1972. On 5 September, several Israeli athletes were taken hostage by a group of Palestinians who said they were from an organisation known as the Black September Organisation (so named as a reminder of the time when Palestinians were massacred in Jordan in September 1970). The terrorists murdered eleven Israeli athletes as well as a German policeman. Five of the eight Palestinians died in the attack, too. Tactics like hijackings and hostage-taking did very little to advance the cause of Palestinian independence and they were eventually abandoned. But some Palestinians, particularly the people who live in Gaza, still believe that the only way to recover their occupied territories is to carry on attacking Israeli citizens. Which is why in the summer of 2014, Palestinians living in blockaded Gaza took action and fired missiles that fell in southern Israel. This time the group responsible was Hamas, an Islamist group that broke away from the non-religious Palestinian authority. Israel reacted by carrying out intensive bombing raids, which according to United Nations statistics left 2,104 Palestinians dead, including 493 children. Seventy Israelis, including six civilians, also died.

'Most politicians in France, and some sections of the press, consider the Palestinians to be terrorists rather than resistance fighters. But not everyone agrees. Yasser Arafat, the leader of the PLO, summed up his view in a speech to the United Nations in November 1974, in which he said: "Anyone who defends a just cause and fights to liberate their country from invaders, occupiers or colonists cannot be called a terrorist." And all along, the Palestinian Authority has continued to believe in negotiating with Israel even though this has never achieved anything.'

'So, with these examples you've been giving, you're saying that terrorism isn't linked specifically to Islam?'

'No, but Islamist terrorism is certainly the most talked about today, partly because it strikes in so many places all over the world. But we shouldn't forget that there have also been massacres of Muslim minorities in many places. Take India and Burma, for example. Muslims were massacred in Gujarat in India in 2002. And in Burma, where Muslims make up about 4 per cent of the population, there was a massacre of Muslims in March 2013. In China, there are places where there is a significant Muslim minority, some of whom agitate for separation from China. Uighur Muslim separatists carried out an attack on passengers at the railway station in Kunming in March 2014 and killed twenty-nine people. But you're right, not all terrorists have historically been associated with Islam.'

'And Hamas. Are they resistance fighters or terrorists?'

'They don't consider themselves to be terrorists. Hamas in Gaza is a group that's inspired by religion, as I said; they're Palestinians resisting occupation in the name of Islam. But as I said before, Palestinians aren't all Islamists! There are Palestinians who are Christian, atheist, non-religious and so on. You may disapprove of what Hamas does, but you should never forget that the people of Gaza are living under a blockade. There's absolutely no reason why they should be expected to accept the expansion of Israeli settlements. Yes, Hamas fights "in the name of Islam", but that's because Islam is a unifying force. It brings people together.'

'Why doesn't Israel remember that Jews once carried out terrorist attacks against the British?'

'From the moment the State of Israel refused to accept the validity of the Palestinian cause, Palestinian fighters were stripped of all legitimacy. Israel rejected their claims, and from then on, they were cast as terrorists and became anathema.'

'What's anathema?'

'It's something or someone that's been condemned, sentenced. It means being cursed, blamed, excluded.'

'That's harsh! What about other Islamist groups?'

'There's a barbaric group called Boko Haram in Nigeria. Boko Haram means literally "forbidden book". Acting in the name of Islam, with a name like that! The mind boggles. They were the ones that took 276 high-school girls hostage in Chibok in northern Nigeria on 14 April 2014. Some of those girls were sold as sex slaves. Boko Haram have kidnapped at least 2,000 women and girls to supply their sex slave trade; Amnesty International puts the number of their victims at more than 4,000.'

'Does Islam authorise terrorism?'

'Of course not. No religion condones the killing of innocent people. The Islam that Boko Haram claims to represent has nothing to do with the religion of the Prophet Muhammad. Nowhere does Islam say to kidnap young girls and sell them into slavery. There have been terrible things done in the name of other religions, too. In France there were the Wars of Religion in the sixteenth century, between Catholics and Protestants, when large numbers of innocent people were slaughtered. You can see illustrations in history books of the tortures that Protestants inflicted on Catholics. And during the Inquisition, Catholics tortured and killed people who weren't Catholics. So-called heretics were burnt at the stake. All three of the monotheistic religions have carried out this kind of slaughter in the name of their religion. But there is no religion that accepts this kind of thing.

'But to get back to what's going on today, Boko Haram have aligned themselves with Daesh, whose atrocities in Syria and Iraq and elsewhere have outdone even Boko Haram. Daesh recognises a man named al-Baghdadi[3] as its leader; he's the one who

---

3   On 27 October 2019 Abu Bakr al-Baghdadi killed himself by detonating a suicide vest while surrounded in a US army raid in northwestern Syria. He is succeeded at the head of Daesh by Abu Ibrahim al-Hashimi al-Qurayshi.

has declared himself to be the caliph of the so-called "Islamic State".'

'I remember the *Charlie Hebdo* killers shouted: "We have avenged the Prophet!", when they murdered the journalists. And the Bataclan killers yelled: "Allahu Akbar". Why did they say those things?'

'It's a signature. They claim to be acting in the interests of Islam, to spread it around the world, when in fact they know nothing about Islam. They've been indoctrinated to pledge their allegiance to al-Baghdadi and quote verses from the Qur'an that supposedly justify their actions. Al-Baghdadi was a prisoner in Iraq at one time and what he wants to do is establish a state based on sharia law and Wahhabism.'

'What do you mean by sharia and Wahhabism?'

'Sharia is a group of rules and laws that a Muslim society is supposed to live by. It includes things like cutting off the hand of a thief, for example, or stoning a woman accused of adultery. Wahhabism refers to the doctrine of a man named Muhammad Ibn Abd al-Wahhab (1703–92), an eighteenth-century theologian who lived in Arabia. It's a harsh and distorted dogma that stems from the tenets of Islam and promotes rigorous application of sharia.'

'So what is it that al-Baghdadi actually wants?'

'He wants to "re-establish the City of God". He's quite willing to behead people he deems to be infidels and display them in front of the world's cameras in order to instil terror all over the world. He is a Sunni and his ultimate goal is to ensure Sunni supremacy in all Arab-Muslim countries, even though there are many Muslims around the world who aren't Sunnis.'

'But why do they have to kill innocent people?'

'Daesh fighters think they're killing heretics, whether they're at the Syrian front or somewhere in Europe. The more unbelievers they kill, the closer they get to paradise, or so they believe!'

'What's a heretic?'

'Someone who doesn't believe. Religions all rely on faith and absolute belief; a heretic refuses to take it all on faith.'

'But why do they have to kill people who don't believe?'

'They think they have to do it to please God!'

'But God doesn't authorise people to slaughter innocent victims, does He?'

'Of course not, but as far as the jihadists are concerned, heretics and unbelievers aren't innocent: the *Charlie Hebdo* team were sentenced to death for blasphemy, for having "insulted" the Prophet. The young people in the Bataclan were punished for their way of life. The killers considered the people at the concert to be decadent, and therefore enemies of Islam. And because Islam must be spread all over the world, anyone who might stand in the way has to be eliminated.'

'And they're willing to die, too. Why?'

'They're not simply ready to sacrifice their own lives, they actively want to die. They believe that life on Earth is not important; what they're interested in is the life in the hereafter, as promised by God, when they'll be able to enjoy the fruits of paradise forever. They see death as the best way to be transported to paradise, a decisive moment when there's no need for fear or hesitation. They offer themselves up to divine will, come what may. They want nothing more than to die.'

'What makes them think like that? How do they get to that point?'

'Someone once said that people whose lives are devoid of meaning turn to death to find meaning. There are so many factors at play when a young person is led down the path of jihadism, it makes it all but impossible for the police or parents to forestall disaster. Fortunately not all young people who think their lives are meaningless get involved in jihad. But young people who are psychologically damaged are vulnerable. The more damaged they are, the more likely they are to fall for the propaganda on the internet – propaganda that gets more varied and convincing all the time. They're more likely to be drawn to the promises that are made, more vulnerable to the call to "change their lives". Finding religious faith, worshipping "heroes" who fight for a cause – it gives them something to dream about. Or perhaps it's just that their day-to-day lives are dreary, they feel hemmed in, frustrated. Jihadist fantasies can give them a structure and make them feel valued. If the good life seems out of reach, whether you live in Europe or an Arab country plagued by economic difficulties, you're going to look elsewhere. Perhaps they're searching for a safe haven, somewhere they can feel at home, "at peace". Or else committing to jihad can be a way of acquiring status, a social promotion that comes with an identity that's tangible and productive. It could be a way of avoiding failure at school, at home or professionally. And by "serving Islam", they can avoid all this. The answer to all their problems is to embrace a destiny that purports to be grand and noble, one that involves fighting in the name of God and "in the way of Allah" *(Fi Sabili Allah)*.'

'Go on.'

'Most of the young people lured into jihadism come from Muslim families, and they're usually aged between fifteen and twenty-five.'

'What, twenty-five-year-olds?'

---

The People of the House (*Ahl al Bayt*)

Aside from the proponents of crude propaganda, there are those who glorify the notion of being one of the 'People of the House', in other words of entering into the House of God, where God's mercy abounds and the believer can live in perfect harmony with the spirit of peace, the spirit of Islam itself. The implication is that those who make the ultimate sacrifice will attain the very essence of purity (*ayn al-tahâra*) and that all the martyrs, all those who have fought 'in the way of

> God' (*Fi Sabili Allah*) will dwell in the House of God and will therefore be purified.
>
> The men who spread these ideas shore up their promises with quotations from the Qur'an and the Hadiths (collected sayings of the Prophet). They manage to make it all seem very convincing to those people who are seeking a path to salvation in a society that has no place for them and offers them virtually no prospects.

'Yes, some people take a long time to grow up. It's tough, being a teenager; dealing with sexual feelings, craving acceptance from peers. For boys, there's the whole question of what it means to be a man. Does it mean being powerful and dominant, being looked up to by younger boys? Some young men get drawn to gang leaders or other father figures, especially if their own father is absent or neglectful. Or they bully their sisters, often with their mother's approval. There's the temptation of drugs, of getting involved with drug-dealing and making easy money. And then they're exposed to the speeches they hear in the mosques, calling for jihad. They, too, can become a "glorious hero" and bask in the light of media attention. There are plenty of girls and young women who fall for these future terrorists. Once upon a time, young men would get themselves noticed by simply going off the rails or getting into trouble with the law. They'd turn into hard men, be a big shot, unafraid of going to jail.

Nowadays, they get attention by opting for jihad and being seen as a hero, or even becoming a "martyr", the ultimate accolade.'

'Go on. Tell me more.'

'For some of the jihadists, death is not an ending, it's the beginning of something else, a way of gaining access to a purer life, in line with the values inherent in the Qur'an and in the Prophet's pronouncements. As they see it, they are entering a world that's wholly devoted to righteousness, a life that's perfect and eternal. They've had enough of this world, they think it's corrupt and not conducive to a pure, healthy life. They want something else, a different way of living, a place where they can fit in and achieve recognition. They don't care if the price for all this is their own death.'

'But not all troubled teenagers join Daesh, do they!'

'No, you're right, they don't. But you can't ignore the influence of online propaganda. Just imagine, Daesh has more than 46,000 Twitter accounts, on top of which they publish at least a thousand documents a month on the internet. They post videos of everyday life, scenes of children at play and veiled women who seem quite content. And then all of a sudden, up comes the battle against "kafirs", against heretics and unbelievers. Young people who live in Europe are told that another life is possible, a life devoted to God. The images are carefully chosen, with the power to fascinate and seduce, rather like those car ads, where an ordinary man is transformed into a superhero driving a luxury car. They play on clichés, stereotyped images that tap into a vulnerable person's deepest longings. Before long that person makes a move, and their friends and family know nothing about it.'

'Why doesn't the government just close down these Twitter accounts?'

'I don't think they can do that. We live in a democracy. The state can't just shut down Twitter accounts from one day to the next, nor any other online platforms.'

'And that's all it takes to get people to sign up for jihad? Online propaganda?'

'No, as I said there are several factors at work. But the grim nature of some people's lives makes them vulnerable to this fascination with extremism: people who live in countries in Europe, North Africa and the Middle East where traditional values are being whittled away and there is no clear vision, no real hope for the future.'

'You mean countries where there's no shared idea of the perfect life?'

'Yes. Once upon a time there was a dream of a free, caring society that was fair and prosperous. It was what the political parties of the left used to talk about. But they've all failed to deliver it. The utopian dream is a thing of the past. And nowadays, increasing numbers of young people in Europe are drawn towards the rhetoric of the extreme right. There may be relatively few of them but they are a dangerous minority. Young people fall prey to all kinds of wild schemes. They seem to have lost faith in values like solidarity, justice, humanitarianism and so forth.'

'What do you mean by utopian dream?'

'The utopian society is an ideal, an imaginary, perfect society that seems impossible to attain. Often, that's all it is: a dream, an illusion.'

'And that's what Daesh offers people? Utopia?'

'More than that. Daesh promises to give meaning to their lives: the chance to lead a life of honour in accordance with sharia. It promises a society that's purified, free of all corruption, an ideal world that is strong and virtuous. A world in which a woman's place is determined by principles that pander to the jihadists' narcissism. Woman is considered to be man's inferior; she must obey him and accommodate his wishes. And if a jihadist dies in combat, he becomes a martyr to be welcomed by God into paradise. A hero, a man of courage. It's a well-thought-out pitch and it works!'

'The thing I just can't understand is that girls and young women get involved in jihad when they know very well that according to sharia, women have a lower status than men. Why?'

'Women never used to fight in battle alongside men. There were women who volunteered to fight in the early days, in the Battle of Badr on 17 March 624. That was when Muhammad won his first victory against the Quraish, the tribe that had driven him into exile in Medina. But the Prophet categorically refused to allow the women to take part in that war. Muhammad's wise advice seems to have been forgotten by the jihadists; not only do they allow women to take up jihad, they actively encourage them to murder innocent people. And jihadist leaders exploit women sexually; they claim it's the "Islamic way" and women believe them. Any women who do rebel are severely punished, or even executed for "treason".'

'So why do they do it? Why do women join Daesh?'

'That's a good question. They're not told the whole truth, and they certainly aren't told how they'll be treated once they get there.'

'How can you identify the people who might become jihadists? Is it possible to spot them before they leave for the front or carry out an atrocity like the 2015 attacks in Paris?'

'You can't tell anything from the way they look. Some of them used to change the way they dressed and let their beards grow. They'd start declaring their allegiance to Islam and being intolerant towards women. But that's all changed now, and these days not even parents can see it coming, let alone the police. The transformation is both subtle and radical. A mother gets a phone call out of the blue from her daughter, who she thought was on a school ski-trip, announcing that she's in Syria, where she's finally found what she was searching for. Just like that. It happens all too often.'

'So there must be some secret motivation, don't you think? Something that no one can see?'

'The Western media sometimes like to make out that the kids who go are nihilistic or insane. But they're not, they're perfectly sane.'

'Can you remind me what nihilistic means?'

'Nihilism, as I explained before, is a completely negative and hopeless doctrine that rejects morality and any system of values at all. Albert Camus described it in his essay *The Rebel* as "a desire to despair and reject".'

'I remember now. You said that jihadists aren't like that. They're not people in absolute despair?'

'That's right. They're not necessarily desperate. But there's something about Islamist jihad that touches a chord in some young people. It appeals to their conscience: there's almost always a vision of some kind behind their murderous attacks. You often hear people say that the spiritual side of life has been sidelined here in Europe. There's a feeling that in the West, materialism counts for more than spiritual values. Young men may feel they're without a voice; perhaps they've been imprisoned for minor offences and feel excluded from society. If you're already deeply disillusioned, the idea of putting God above everything else can be very appealing. Life on Earth becomes nothing but a stage on the road towards life in heaven. People are happy to believe in an all-powerful God, a God who is the beginning and end of all things, to accept that our destiny is in God's hands.

They think they'll achieve the ideal of returning to God if they answer the call to jihad. There's an expression Muslims often use when someone is agitated and upset: "Come back to God!" In other words: "There's no point in getting all wound up. If you come back to God, He'll solve all your problems." What they mean is that before God, we are very small indeed. And God is merciful and forgiving.'

'So, they think they're going back to where they came from?'

'Not exactly. They're not going backwards, but to quote the poet René Char, they're going "back uphill", going from the limited period of time here on Earth up to the eternity of heaven. It means they no longer have to think for themselves; the absolute certainties of belief will take away all doubt and anguish. The Word of God provides for everything. And it's not just troubled youngsters who join Daesh. There are people who don't have any particular problems, law-abiding people earning a living, with steady jobs, who give up everything to join Daesh. They think they'll be guaranteed a life of excitement; they will be soldiers of God, ready to carry out terrorist acts.'

'I've seen video clips of children being taught to shoot the "enemy".'

'I know, we've all seen those horrifying images. And yet the Prophet always insisted children shouldn't be involved in war. At the Battle of Badr in the early days of Islam, there were adolescents who lied about their age so they could fight, but the Prophet found them out and sent them home.'

***

'I'm lost. Can we recap, please! What exactly is a terrorist?'

'Someone who goes into battle in order to spread terror. But there are many different kinds of terrorist violence, as well as various kinds of violence that aren't necessarily terrorism-related: for example, political violence in support of dubious causes, or violence carried out in the name of a religion. But whatever the cause, terrorist violence involves targeting public places in the full knowledge that innocent people will die. Or it could mean targeting an important person, such as a minister, a union leader, a head of state, or a well-known thinker. Sometimes the target is a monument or a place of symbolic importance. But the goal is always to spread fear and chaos. And in doing this, terrorists break the social contract that enables people to live together whatever their differences. They step outside the framework of civilisation, if you like, the framework of law and order.

'Terrorists are people whose aim is to terrorise the population. They have chosen to do what they do, knowing that they will kill people they don't know and who've done them no harm. They have clearly defined notions of good and evil that lead them to opt for this means of action.'

'Are they insane?'

'No, they're not. A mad person isn't responsible for their actions. But terrorists know exactly what they are doing; they've been trained by experts to kill and be killed. They aren't always given full information, but they're willing to submit themselves to their superiors and obey orders.'

'Aren't they scared?'

'No, and that makes them hard to defeat. Usually, in a war, enemies confront each other and troops from the two sides battle it out. But now, with jihadism, war has a new face. Jihadist soldiers aren't necessarily defending territory or property. And they are prepared to lose their lives, which is what gives them their greatest strength.'

'Why do they agree to give up their own lives killing other people?'

'All living beings have a survival instinct, the natural desire to protect yourself, to stay alive. An instinct for self-preservation. It's something human beings have in common with animals. Terrorists who blow themselves up in a crowd have swapped their survival instinct for a death wish.'

'How can that be?'

'They're lied to by men who are experts in manipulating people's minds to the point where their victims are willing to carry out any instructions they're given. The stories they tell them aren't based on rational thinking.'

'Give me some examples.'

'They use words that fit with what they're aiming to achieve: words like jihad, martyr, paradise, supreme reward. It's religious terminology. Sometimes, for a believer, passing from this world to the next doesn't seem so difficult. So these terrorists are willing to believe that if they practise jihad and wage war on unbelievers, on people who don't believe in their God, if they give up their own lives in sacrifice, they'll go straight to paradise where beautiful virgins, a thousand times more beautiful than here on Earth, will be waiting for them. And then there are the images you see on the internet, of heroic fighters laden with weapons, big strong men, armed to the teeth. They're fascinated by all this – and these are symbols of manhood, too.'

'Wow! And what about the girls? What rewards are they promised?'

'That's a good question. People think only boys and men are drawn to jihad and martyrdom. But about a third of jihadists are young women, even though, as I explained earlier, neither the Prophet nor his followers accepted the idea of women going to war. Neither women nor children, obviously. And yet as you know, Daesh recruits women to use as they see fit and turns children into killers.'

'So what is there for a young woman to get out of waging holy war?'

'I suppose the idea that she'll go to heaven, but Islamists despise women so much that they won't even discuss this. There's the promise that she'll be a martyr; they seem to think that's reward enough!'

'Becoming a martyr – what does it mean?'

'Being a martyr means dying for a cause, an ideal, and therefore being worthy of a reward chosen by God. It says in the Qur'an that those who die fighting in the way of God will not die. Instead they'll be "martyrs" destined for heaven.'

'And there's no truth in any of this?'

'There is for a person who believes in it – it's not merely the truth, it's the absolute truth. So long as they believe they'll be a martyr, that's all that matters. From that point on, they're cut off from reality as we know it, they've removed themselves from the world the rest of us live in. They see life on Earth as a passing phase; that's why they agree so readily to die. It's also what makes them so dangerous. They look on death as a moment of glory.'

'What do you mean by a moment of glory?'

'The moment when all your dreams are realised. To achieve this through jihad means you'll experience boundless joy; the moment of death opens the way to paradise.'

'What can we do to avoid running into these people?'

'We usually tell children to be careful. But what do we mean by that? The people at the Bataclan in November 2015 had no reason to think they'd lose their lives there. Surprise is a powerful weapon. There's no such thing as 100 per cent guaranteed security. The police work hard; what they do is essential and very important. But education is important, too, and on no account should it be neglected. It's often racism that lies at the heart of fanaticism and intolerance, two things that can lead to the spread of terror and murder of innocent people. Schools need to integrate the battle against racism into their curriculum; the educational system hasn't exactly been successful at doing this.'

'You mean schools haven't done enough to prevent the rise of terrorism in France?'

'Perhaps not. But they have to be part of the equation, don't you think?'

'It seems to me you're saying this is a war we can't win...'

'This is a war that has to be waged on several fronts. Yes, we have to bomb jihadist army bases, dismantle their training camps, destroy their stockpiles of arms and cut off their sources of funding. But there are sleeper cells in Europe and around the world, groups of individuals waiting for the order to strike, and none of this will have much impact on them. We have to do everything we can to get to the bottom of this very dangerous phenomenon. As de Gaulle said, it's no good going to the "complicated Orient with simple ideas". These are young people, here in Europe, who don't feel integrated, who don't feel this is their country. Some of them don't feel as if they belong here.'

'Why not?'

'There have been several decades of serious neglect. There's been no coherent policy. Whole generations of immigrants and the sons and daughters of immigrants have been abandoned, left to rot at the margins of society, in pernicious circumstances that offer no hope for the future.'

'What do you mean by pernicious?'

'A toxic environment that doesn't allow a person to make the most of themselves. A lawless environment the police prefer to avoid.'

'Are you talking about the *banlieues*, the immigrant suburbs? Are you saying they're unhealthy places?'

'Yes, that's right. Some of the kids say things like: "The West wanted to make us disappear; we were supposed to assimilate or be satisfied with being left by the wayside." Youngsters feel hemmed in on all sides: failing at school, cut off from education because their parents are unable to give them the support they need, thwarted by racism in the job market. And that's when Islam steps in and claims to "save" them: a skilled recruiter manages to convince them that there is another way, a way that leads to absolute purity, to a world governed by the word of God. Talk of a return to divine certainties can seem like a gift to these kids. It makes them feel safe and offers them a way out. The secular notion of freedom of conscience can't hold up against the Islamist agenda. So they sign up for it and commit to it. And the ones that come back from the battlefields of Syria and Iraq are the most dangerous of all; they're ready to strike at any moment without warning as soon as they're given the order. And to complete the picture, their parents have been powerless and ill-prepared to deal with any of this. They've been unable to pass on any humanistic values of peace to their children. It wouldn't be right to blame parents entirely, but they do bear some responsibility in all of this.'

'Why are the people who've returned from the battlefields the most dangerous?'

'Because they're invisible, scattered here and there; they're hard to spot. There's nothing special about their appearance. They blend into the crowd, they can't be singled out and picked up by the police. Remember, France is a society in which people have civil rights; the police can't just arrest anyone at random on suspicion of being a danger to society. The law must be respected, even with the state of emergency.'

'Give me an example.'

'Have you heard of the "white caliph"? He's a Syrian who came to France in the 1970s fleeing repression from Hafez al-Assad (Bashar al-Assad's father) and his police. He goes by the name of Olivier Corel. He's a member of the Muslim Brotherhood, a group founded in 1928 in Egypt with the aim of promoting the spread of Islam around the world. He acquired French nationality and gradually became the spiritual leader of a number of would-be jihadists, some of whom, like Mohammed Merah, went on to commit appalling crimes in France. Like the rest of the Muslim Brotherhood, this so-called white caliph harboured ideas about the expansion of Islam; they believe that one day, Islam will reign throughout the world. When the police searched his house, all they found was an old hunting rifle that wasn't registered. He was given a suspended sentence of seven months imprisonment. Everyone knows the police think he is the man who inspires and recruits terrorists in France, but the law is powerless against him unless they can catch him red-handed committing an illegal act.'

'Tell me how these men you're talking about manage to manipulate people so successfully.'

'It's a combination of things. There are many factors involved in turning someone into a kamikaze, hoping to die a martyr.'

'What's a kamikaze?'

'It was a word used in the Second World War. Kamikazes were Japanese suicide bombers, enlisted soldiers who were following orders. They only attacked precise military targets. It wasn't seen as suicide – death was part of their job, and they had no alternative but to accept it. It only happened during the war. But the jihadists are different from the Japanese kamikaze pilots. Jihadists are civilians, signed up to a political and religious cause, deliberately targeting fellow civilians. The idea of sacrificing your own life like this is virtually unheard-of in a civilised society; our survival instinct won't allow it. And suicide is roundly condemned by Islam, even for a cause that claims to be "noble".'

'And is the same true for being a martyr?'

'It's not quite the same thing. When someone dies for a cause at the hands of an enemy, they're seen as a martyr, battling in "the way of God". And in that case, God promises them paradise. But you have to be a believer.'

'A Muslim, you mean?'

'Yes, and Islam only advocates what people call jihad in exceptional circumstances: for example, when the faithful are attacked by enemy troops. That was what happened during the Crusades, when the Christians waged war against the Muslims. The faithful who died at the hands of the Christians were seen as martyrs. The Qur'an is quite clear on this. Those who give their lives for God in battle don't die; they live forever, in heaven.'

'Did the Bataclan terrorists want to go to heaven?'

'Probably, but they committed crimes that Islam doesn't sanction. There's a verse in the Qur'an that says unequivocally: "The man who kills an innocent person, kills all of humanity." They are murderers, that's all. They're not martyrs and they're not Muslims. There's an instruction in the Hadith, the sayings of the Prophet, given to fighters preparing to go into battle against the enemies of Islam at Mu'tah: "Go in the name of Allah. Do battle against the enemies of Allah who are also your enemies. In Syria, you will encounter monks living in their cells, far away from other people; do not trouble them. You will find warriors devoted to Satan; fight against them, sword in hand. Do not kill any women, children or old people. Do not fell a single palm or any other tree. Do not destroy a single house."'

'But I've heard people say that all this violence is part of Islam. Is that true?'

'Every religion has a violent side. Belief is not a rational thing, and emotions often win out. Many people have fought in God's name throughout history and none of the major religions have avoided wars being waged in their name. For example, as I mentioned before, the Catholics in France persecuted and slaughtered the Protestants in the sixteenth century. As for Islam, it all depends on the way you read and interpret the religious texts. Islam was the last of the revealed monotheistic religions to be founded, and there were battles, wars and violence in response to those who refused to accept the message brought by the Prophet Muhammad. One verse in the Qur'an says: "Kill the infidels wherever you find them. Take them captive, besiege them and ambush them." But it was an order given at a particular time in a specific set of circumstances, in Medina, at the end of the Prophet's life.'

'You're contradicting yourself! First you quote from the verse that condemns the person who kills an innocent person and then you cite this other verse that says: "Kill the infidels!"'

'The first quote holds for all time and all places, the other is specific to the context of a war at a particular time, a war waged against the new prophet by those who didn't accept his message.'

'Is that what's behind the current violence?'

'No, not exactly. But modern jihadists are certainly convinced that slaughtering innocent people in Paris, Beirut, Tunisia, Syria and Iraq is justified. They see it as no different from fighting to defend the Prophet when he was forced to leave Medina to escape the "infidels" who wanted him dead. They're told to believe we're still living in the seventh century, or at least that those days are still relevant today.'

'But they know perfectly well this is the twenty-first century!'

'Yes, but they don't think like us: you have to understand that these people don't value earthly life above all else; what matters to them is the afterlife. They firmly believe that God determines everything, that it's all written in advance. Man is nothing but an instrument in the hands of divine power, so if they have to die, they won't protest and they won't be afraid.'

'Do you think they are real believers?'

'I have no idea, but why would they do these things if they didn't believe? They are obeying what they think is an order from on high, even though that order is actually given by men who are manipulating them and telling them what to do. They're not insane; they're people who think they've finally found the light they've waited a long time for. And how do you explain the well-educated young Europeans who take up jihad? They're not delinquents or drug addicts. Their actions come as a great surprise to everyone, especially their parents who would never in their wildest dreams have imagined that one day their children would convert in secret and go off to Syria or Iraq to join a jihadist army.'

'And this light they've found leads them to kill!'

'They don't see their actions as evil. The orders they're carrying out come from a world view that's been inculcated into them by professional jihadists. They believe they're carrying out a mission that will grant them redemption, a mission that will save their soul.'

'So what exactly is jihad then?'

'In times of peace, jihad is the effort each of us must put in to better ourselves and be a good Muslim, a person who does all they can to do good and stand up against evil and injustice. The Qur'an requires this of us. In times of war, jihad means the battle against the enemies of Islam. It's the battle in the "way of God": you fight for the divine message to triumph. You're ready to give your life to advance that ideal. But nowadays, there's no serious threat to Islam; quite the opposite. Islam is continuing to spread in spite of all the bad press it gets.'

'So how do they get these young people to buy into the idea that we're at war?'

'It's about getting them to believe we're still living in the time of the revelation of Islam as the religion destined to save all of humanity. To believe the battle isn't over yet, it still hasn't been won. It's ironic that the ones doing the manipulating of young people's minds happen to make use of the most modern and sophisticated of twenty-first-century techniques. Their propaganda machine is fearsomely effective: striking images, videos of battle scenes, endlessly replayed audio messages, non-stop chanting of particular verses from the Qur'an, scenes from daily life showing what looks like real camaraderie. It all has a powerful effect on the person watching; they get drawn in and succumb to the message, all critical faculties forgotten. The aim is to utterly destroy freedom of thought in the minds of future jihadists. Instead of thinking for themselves, they have to submit completely and agree to do whatever they're asked to do. It's no different from the way cults operate. They use the same methods to control their followers.'

'It's a form of marketing.'

'Exactly! It's a carefully calculated method for taking control of people's minds in order to manipulate them. It's indoctrination. The subjects are taught a few basic concepts and made to repeat them over and over again until in the end, those concepts are firmly entrenched as the one and only truth. It's an extremely effective form of instruction.'

'Yes but how do you explain what that boy from Marseille did in 2016? The one who went out with a machete one day in January, completely out of the blue, intending to go and "kill some Jews"? He was well brought up, wasn't he, a good student, from a Turkish family of Kurdish origins?'

'That boy was barely sixteen years old. He'd learnt about the "Islamic State" from the internet. Neither his parents nor his teachers noticed him being radicalised. He came across the jihadist propaganda that's all over the internet. In prison he showed no remorse at all; he claimed to be a supporter of Isis and said the only thing he regretted was that "the victim didn't die"! What can you do against that kind of behaviour? It's hard to combat this kind of terrorism. The boy had clearly been inculcated with such hatred by jihadist propaganda but we don't know what tipped him over into actually committing an act of murder.'

'So what can we do to counteract all this propaganda?'

'To do it properly, you'd have to clean up the internet, which is virtually impossible. You can't just turn off the internet tap – it isn't only a tool for criminal propaganda, and this is a democratic society. We talked about this before with regard to Twitter. Parents have to be extremely vigilant and keep an eye on the kind of images their children are seeing online. It's very difficult, I know, and that's why it's essential to always be able to communicate openly with your children. Parents have to take time to talk to their children, explain things to them, help them to understand and warn them of dangers. Above all, parents must trust their children and give them a sense of responsibility, especially when they're teenagers. And schools and the media have to play their part, too.'

'I read on an internet site that anti-Semitism was rife among Islamist terrorists. What's to be done about racism like that?'

'Well, in 2016, after that boy tried to murder Jews in Marseille, some rabbis asked Jewish people to stop wearing the kippa, as a way of protecting themselves from being identified and attacked. But that's no solution. The problem goes much deeper. Anti-Semitism has existed in France and all over Europe for a long time. Take the Dreyfus Affair, for example. Dreyfus was a Jewish officer in the French army who was accused of treason at the beginning of the twentieth century. The whole country was split over the affair, with one side being violently anti-Semitic and the other anti-racist. Dreyfus's most famous supporter was the novelist Emile Zola. And of course you know about the Holocaust, the tragic fate of Europe's Jews under the Nazis. But the modern version of anti-Jewish sentiment among jihadists is different. It harks back to Wahhabi dogma and the conflict that developed at the time of the Prophet Muhammad, between 622 and 632, when the Muslims accused the Jews of Medina of having broken a pact they'd made with the Prophet. Jihadists and their mentors can't let go of the idea that back then, the Prophet was betrayed by the Jews. And that idea has been updated to become part of fundamentalist dogma today. This is the kind of thing they've been teaching young Muslims in religious schools all over the world for decades, in madrasas often built and funded by

Wahhabis from Saudi Arabia. The Saudis have been responsible for building and providing materials for more than 1,500 madrasas all over the world, but particularly in Pakistan and Afghanistan.'

'So it all dates back to the birth of Islam?'

'Yes, but in Andalusia, it didn't stop Jews and Muslims from living peacefully side by side for hundreds of years, right up until the start of the Inquisition in the fifteenth century when they fled to Morocco and other Muslim countries. Even then, they continued to live alongside one another without any problems until 1948, when the State of Israel was created.'

'Aren't there laws in France that punish incitement to racial hatred?'

'Yes, there are laws condemning both racism and anti-Semitism, but they have little effect on the people who are driven by hatred. Islamist propaganda lays great stress on "hatred of Jews". Merah, Nemmouche and Coulibaly all attacked Jews. As they saw it, Jews were responsible for the suffering of Muslims in Palestine and Israel.'

'So what's to be done about this kind of propaganda?'

'Jews and Muslims would have to agree to fight it together – hatred of Jews and hatred of Muslims are similar evils. Serious questions would need to be asked. And of course it wouldn't be easy. It's not enough just to be educated. People need to read and be curious and outward-looking, interested in other cultures. Parents have to talk to their children and make them eager to use their imagination and learn about the world. They have to teach them to question everything. And then they have to steer their children away from the voices that shout the loudest and neglect humanitarian values. They have to warn them against seductive, deceptive images. The propaganda of hate can be powerful and insidious, and parents have to be constantly on the alert.'

'Dad, I'm going to ask you something you'll find annoying. I know lots of people ask you this, but tell me, why are so many people scared of Islam? Are they right to be scared?'

'Well, first of all, when you say Islam, which form of Islam are you talking about?'

'You mean there are different sorts of Islam?'

'No, but Islam is based on written texts and there are several different ways of understanding those texts. Islam is what we call a monotheistic religion – it only has one God, Allah, who is unique and all-powerful, as you know. It shares its roots with Judaism and Christianity, the other two monotheistic religions. There have always been different and sometimes contradictory ways of understanding Islam. That's true of other religions, too. So, yes, there are some Muslims who want to drag Islam towards violence. They've read the texts but they haven't grasped the basics of Islamic thought or understood the subtleties. They twist what it says. And then there are all the Muslims who go about their lives in peace, the Muslims who believe in moderation. But you never hear about those people in the news. The only Muslims you see are the ones bent on violence.'

'Yes, but people lump all Muslims together. They're frightened of Islam because individuals who call themselves Muslims think nothing of murdering those they consider to be infidels. So really, people are right to be scared, aren't they?'

'You can't just reduce Islam to images of horrible murders committed in the name of Muhammad. You're right to be angry. Of course you are. But don't forget: for the last thirty years or so, most of the victims of violent Islamism have been Muslims themselves.'

'So why are there no Muslim leaders standing up and condemning all these murderers?'

'Because Sunni Islam isn't organised the way the Christian church is. There's no pope or archbishop, there aren't even any priests. The faithful answer directly to God. In Shia Islam, the other branch of Islam, there is an organised structure: Shia Muslims revere Ali, the Prophet's son-in-law as the first true imam and they have mullahs, ayatollahs, muftis and so on. But there's no one to speak out in the name of all Muslims. And after the *Charlie Hebdo* and Bataclan attacks, most Muslims in France did say they were horrified and didn't accept that people should be murdered in the name of Islam. But unfortunately there were no mass demonstrations. Muslims didn't get together and come out on the streets to let people know what they thought of these horrors being committed in their name.

'Every time an attack is carried out in the name of Islam, Muslims feel terrible. It's a serious problem in Muslim society. People know their image will suffer. And, yes, of course there are Muslim scholars who have condemned the attacks. The head of the Al-Azhar University in Cairo spoke out against the attacks, and scholars in Morocco even declared a fatwa against the attacks of 13 November. But, as I've said, their words don't carry the weight of a pope's.'

'So why aren't French Muslims unified?'

'Most Muslims are Sunnis, and as I said, in Sunni Islam, there's no head, no leader; and there's no tradition of organised unity. And even within Sunni Islam itself, there are many different strands, all with their own rites and practices. It makes it very difficult for people to come together and choose a representative to speak for all Muslims. There are too many differences, too many rivalries. It's always been like that, ever since the death of the Prophet Muhammad.'

'French Muslims must have felt awful after the *Charlie Hebdo* and Kosher supermarket attacks in January 2015, and then in the following November, after the Bataclan.'

'Of course they did. Everyone was shocked and devastated by those atrocities. Men and women everywhere were very upset, especially since the *Charlie Hebdo* victims were ordinary journalists.

They were cartoonists, poets, jokers. They weren't full of hate and bigotry. It was their job to make fun of everything and everyone. But there were also some people in France who applauded the murders. Not many, of course, but there were some. The day after the attacks, there was a minute's silence all over France to honour the victims, and in seventy of the 64,000 schools in France there were pupils who refused to join in. It was only a very small number, but you can't ignore it.

'And you also can't ignore the fact that racism against Muslims has become commonplace in France. And not just in France, but all over Europe. Hate crimes against Muslims went up by 500% in France between 2014 and 2015.'

'Speaking of the *Charlie Hebdo* attacks, how do you explain the fact that while all of France was in shock, there were some kids in the *banlieues* who said: "*Je ne suis pas Charlie* – I'm not Charlie?" They said the journalists had it coming; they should have kept their hands off the Prophet.'

'Yes, it's true, there were reports in the press of Muslims who expressed "admiration and even fascination" for the *Charlie Hebdo* killers. You remember the famous slogan, *Je suis Charlie* ("I am Charlie"), but there was an opposite slogan, too, *Je ne suis pas Charlie, je suis Kouachi et Coulibaly* (the names of the killers). And there were others who were quick to declare: "*Je ne suis pas Charlie*", men like Jean-Marie Le Pen, once the leader and then the honorary president of the Front National in France.

'Jamel Guenaoui, a teacher and spokesperson for a group that promotes diversity, spoke to a journalist from the newspaper *Le Figaro* about the kids who identify with the killers. In an interview of 14 January 2015 he said: "These kids don't know what they're saying. They're full of unbelievable hate. They need a change of environment if they're to learn to be more accepting of others and of themselves. As it is, they're lost, they're ready to follow the first hero that comes along, the first orator." The publication of cartoons of the Prophet Muhammad gave them an excuse to protest. It was a way of claiming their Muslim identity.

'That's why I keep saying we have to get to the root of the problem. Kids in immigrant communities have been marginalised and neglected, and they've become completely cut off. They're shut up in a narrow little world, with its own laws and rules. There are some neighbourhoods the police won't go into, largely because they don't think this would serve any purpose and also because they consider the area to be too dangerous.

'What do kids like that know about Islam?'

'Nothing, or virtually nothing. Snippets of verses, a few catchphrases to back up what they believe. They're full of hate. And in the summer of 2014 during the Israeli bombing of Gaza, when they heard French president François Hollande and prime minister Manuel Valls giving Israel their unqualified support, their hatred no doubt doubled in intensity. After the January 2015 attacks in Paris, some kids were reported as saying: "Why should we observe a minute's silence for a few Jews when no one observed a minute's silence for the Palestinians last summer?" The government's support for Israeli actions feeds the defiant attitude these young people harbour towards France. Some of them identify with the Palestinian cause in the same way many Jewish people do with the State of Israel. They feel a strong sense of injustice: they consider that Palestinians aren't treated with as much compassion as Israeli soldiers. There's a double standard. The Israeli-Palestinian conflict and the way it's treated by politicians and the media are key factors in the breakdown between these young people and the rest of French society. At least, that's what the kids say when they're interviewed. And the comedian Dieudonné's anti-Israel stance has a big influence on them, too. His videos are seen by millions.'[4]

'So let me ask you again: should we be afraid of Islam?'

'Yes, we should fear the men who exploit Islam to fuel their desire to dominate and rule over other

---

[4] Dieudonné M'bala M'bala is a French comedian, actor and political activist. He has been convicted for hate speech, advocating terrorism and slander in Belgium and France. An unrepentant anti-Semite, his friends include Jean-Marie Le Pen and Mahmoud Ahmadinejad, president of Iran from 2005 to 2013. Dieudonné's popularity on social media was at its height in 2016-2017.

people; and yes, jihadists are a threat. How numerous are they? According to the French Ministry of the Interior, there were a total of 8,250 "radicalised individuals" in February 2016, all of them potential jihadists. It's one thing to identify and keep a record of who these people are, but monitoring them day and night is another matter and the French state doesn't have the resources to do that. Around 500 of them have returned from Syria. Whether or not they're repentant is anyone's guess; they may be ticking time bombs for all we know. Some of them are being held, awaiting trial. But imprisoning them won't solve the problem. In prison they'll only be further radicalised.'

'So there really is cause to be afraid...'

'You can certainly see why people in France might be afraid of Islam and Muslims these days. But there are other reasons, too, such as the way women are treated in some Muslim countries. In Saudi Arabia, Pakistan and Iran, for example, women are denied the rights enjoyed by men; practices such as polygamy, divorce by repudiation, even stoning are legally accepted, and when a woman inherits, she receives only half as much as a male. It's a fanatical, ultraconservative worldview that's backed up by the Muslim Brotherhood and its philosophy. The Muslim Brotherhood was founded in 1928 by Hasan al-Banna, an educator in Egypt whose teachings insisted on the superiority of Islam over other religions. He called for society to be Islamised, and said there was a need to take power and create an "Islamic State", in which sharia law could be practised and democratic principles such as individual freedom and secularism contested.'

'So in a way the jihadists of today are inspired by the Muslim Brotherhood?'

'I talked about this in my book *Islam Explained* (New Press, 2004). I've attempted to account for these ideas. Of course, that doesn't mean that I support them; far from it. Europeans find much of sharia law deeply shocking: they're appalled to see how women are treated in some parts of the world. They learn that under sharia law the punishment for theft is to cut off the thief's hand, that a woman convicted of adultery is stoned to death, that apostasy and ordinary crimes are punishable by death by beheading. When people in the West hear these things, they say how much they hate the Islam that condones them.'

'What's apostasy?'

'It means publicly renouncing your religion and declaring yourself an atheist, an unbeliever. In the West, this is a matter for the individual, a question of conscience. But Muslim countries don't recognise freedom of conscience – except for Tunisia, where it is protected by the New Constitution.'

'And the punishment for apostasy is death?'

'Yes, it's considered a capital offence in Saudi Arabia, and in Egypt, too. Ashraf Fayadh, a Palestinian poet living in Saudi Arabia, was condemned to death for apostasy in November 2015. He protested his innocence and made it clear that he's not an atheist, but he's still being held in prison. Hopefully the international outcry surrounding his case will prevent them from actually carrying out the sentence.'[5]

'So you're saying it's understandable that Europeans don't want this kind of Islam taking hold in their countries? I've heard that in Italy, the Lega[6] party's supporters say there's every reason to be worried. They think Muslims should be forced out of Italy. And there was a journalist in France who said that Muslims should be deported. What do you think about those people?'

'Lega in Italy are like National Rally[7] in France, or Pegida (Patriotic Europeans against the Islamicisation of the Occident) in Germany. There are other far-right parties, too: there's the National Democratic Party of Germany, the FPO (Freedom Party of Austria), Vlaams Belang (the Belgian far-right party) and the neo-Nazi Golden Dawn party in Greece. They're all parties of the far right and all of them are anti-immigration, especially Muslim immigration. They play on people's fears without ever explaining the reasons behind immigration. They do it to get voters on their side and it seems to work. They've all been doing very well in elections. In Europe as a whole, far-right parties probably get more than a quarter of the

---

[5] The sentence has since been commuted to eight years in prison and 800 lashes after the international outcry.

[6] Formerly National League, the party changed its name to Lega in 2018.

[7] The National Front in France changed its name to National Rally (*Rassemblement Nationale*) in 2018.

vote, and all because they take advantage of fear of Islam in their campaigns.'

'How did Europe get to this point?'

'Fear! Fear combined with ignorance, prejudice and racism. And on top of all that, the indiscriminate attacks that kill innocent civilians. Terrorism creates a climate of fear everywhere. And politicians have understood that tapping into that fear is a sure way of being elected. Even in countries well known for their generous immigration policies, such as Sweden and Denmark, far-right parties have increased their share of the vote to 25% and 21% respectively by waving the flag of the Muslim threat.'

'Is there really any basis for all this fear?'

'I can understand why people who aren't well informed might be afraid, especially when their security isn't properly guaranteed by their governments. But it's important to realise that it's much easier to stir up fear and anxiety than it is to reassure people. Fear really took hold after the destruction of the Twin Towers in New York in September 2001, when almost 3,000 people were killed. It was an outrage that had a worldwide effect. And in France, it only needed one terrifying attack committed by a young Frenchman of Muslim descent to cast suspicion on all French Muslims. I'm talking about Mohammed Merah, who killed three soldiers in Montauban and four Jewish people, three of them children, in Toulouse in March 2012. Now, since the 2015 attacks, it's become very difficult to restore the image of Islam in France. However much you insist that the principles of Islam have been twisted by ignorant terrorists who know nothing of Islam, people still tend to condemn Islam as a whole. The truth is that people don't make the effort to go beyond appearances and overcome prejudices. In Ajaccio in Corsica, a mosque was attacked on Christmas Eve in 2015 by a crowd chanting "Arabs out" and other racist slogans. It happened during a demonstration against immigration from North Africa. Between 13 November 2015 and the end of that year, the CCIF (Association against Islamophobia in France) counted a total of 222 acts of discrimination against Muslims.'

'So fear of Islam has come about because of terrorism carried out in the name of Islam?'

'Yes, it has. And not only do people fear Islam, they hate it, too. It's become quite acceptable to attack Islam and those who identify as Muslims: the writer Michel Houellebecq for example, has openly expressed his contempt for Islam.'

'All this fear and hatred, it's very worrying.'

'Yes. The *Charlie Hebdo* team were under threat from the moment their cartoons of the Prophet Muhammad were published. Their premises were set fire to in 2011. And then on 7 January 2015 most of them were assassinated by killers shouting: "We have avenged the Prophet." As far as the killers, and the men who manipulated them were concerned, the cartoons were examples of blasphemy, the worst crime of all.'

'Are you talking about the caricatures that were originally published in a Danish newspaper?'

'Yes, and then they were reprinted in *Charlie Hebdo*, which, dare I say, made things worse.'

'And that's why the terrorists murdered those twelve people.'

'Yes, although for the killers, it wasn't just about killing Cabu, Wolinski, Charb and all the others. What they wanted was to spread terror and strike a blow against freedom of expression, against the freedom to write, draw and sing freely, to be ironic, critical or satirical. All that bloodshed for the sake of a joke. Of course, no religion likes being laughed at. But to kill because of that...'

'So, I'm not allowed to make jokes about Islam, or laugh at it, because I'm from a Muslim family.'

'Well, you can joke about it if you like, but not in public in a Muslim country. Here in Europe, you have the right to express yourself freely, whenever and however you want. You can write, draw, paint, sing, it's up to you. No one can take away your right to freedom of expression. Of course, there will always be fanatics ready to make problems for you, but freedom of expression is a basic right in France. It goes back a long way, to Rabelais, Voltaire, Zola and other writers and thinkers from the Renaissance onwards. Satirical writing is a long-standing tradition in France. It's a defining characteristic of this country. And religion has always been a target of the satirists. *Charlie Hebdo* has published dozens of covers over the years, satirising various religious figures, from rabbis to the pope. That's what freedom means.'

'But why did they publish those cartoons? Why make fun of the Prophet revered by more than a billion Muslims? Surely it's provocative to insult and humiliate Muslims like that?'

'Well yes, you could say it was provocative. Or that it was in bad taste. And I can certainly understand why the faithful felt insulted when they saw their Prophet being demeaned. But we live in a country where blasphemy has long been tolerated. France is a secular society. It's fought to keep religion separate from the state, to keep it out of the public sphere, out of education and politics. If you decide to live in France, you have to agree to abide by its laws and to accept its principles and fundamental values.'

'You say that France is a secular society. What exactly does that mean?'

'A law was passed in 1905, separating the church from the state, and since then, France has been a secular society with no official religion. The Christian Church used to say that "France is the Church's elder daughter". But that link was broken in 1905. It doesn't mean that people aren't religious; it's only the state that's secular, not the whole of society. People have the right to practise any religion they choose in complete safety. But religion must be kept out of the public sphere – out of schools, for example. Secularism isn't an attack on religions, it's simply a principle that says religion and politics have to kept separate. Religion is a private matter.

'But in the eyes of the fanatics, secularism is no different from atheism. They see anyone who blasphemes as an apostate and as such someone who must be rejected by the Muslim community: their blood must flow. Those were the Ayatollah Khomeini's very words when he issued a fatwa against Salman Rushdie, who wrote *The Satanic Verses*. That was in 1989, and Rushdie's life is still under threat. The fatwa has never been lifted. Can you imagine? Being threatened with death for having written a novel? It's horrific!'

'So that really is an example of Islam being violent.'

'It's one facet of Islam. But according to the Qur'an, it's God who deals with Muslims who go astray. But we're not talking about God here. Rushdie was being punished by Ayatollah Khomeini, an old man who didn't support freedom of expression, who didn't believe in the right to create, imagine and invent freely. An old man backed by millions of fanatics ready to carry out his fatwa. All Rushdie was doing in his book was telling a story. *The Satanic Verses* wasn't an attack on Islam; it wasn't an essay criticising Islam. But the fatwa called for murder and one of Rushdie's translators was stabbed to death as a result.[8] There

---

8 This was in Japan in 1991. The Italian translator was also wounded.

have been other fatwas, too, declared against other intellectuals and free thinkers.'

'What exactly is a fatwa?'

'It's a religious command. In Sunni Islam, no one actually has the right to take it upon themselves to declare a fatwa against anyone in particular. But religious scholars do in fact make judgements against individuals who in their estimation have "left the house of Islam". And in Shia Islam, some do have the right to issue fatwas, as was the case with Ayatollah Khomeini when he decided to condemn Rushdie to death. But a fatwa is merely a religious command that has no legal or court value. It means nothing in the eyes of the law.'

'How awful! But can I ask you about the Kouachi brothers again, the *Charlie Hebdo* killers? They were French, weren't they? And so were the terrorists of the 13 November attacks in Paris. They were all born in France, their parents were immigrants. Why did they do such terrible things? Why did they commit those barbaric crimes? I understand what you've been saying about being manipulated, but all the same ...'

'Yes, they were French. But did they really feel themselves to be French? They'd been left to their own devices from an early age, uneducated delinquents who never finished school. Some of them had been in prison. They came out empty-headed, or perhaps I should say muddle-headed, the perfect target for jihadist recruiters. They first came into contact with a man named Farid Benyettou, a charismatic mentor who must have made quite an impression on them. No doubt he knew how to find the right words to indoctrinate them. And there were probably others who took charge of brainwashing them and pumping them full of Islamist slogans. Benyettou had spent six years in prison on a charge of criminal conspiracy in connection with a terrorist enterprise. The Paris Tribunal that convicted him in 2008 considered him to be the leader of the Buttes Chaumont terror cell, a group that recruited young people to go and fight in Iraq. Benyettou helped to radicalise the Kouachi brothers, after which they were placed under the leadership of others who armed and trained them to commit attacks in France. We know now that the Kouachi brothers' crimes were claimed by Al-Qaeda in Yemen, and the 13 November 2015 attacks by Daesh.'

'So were the *Charlie Hebdo* and the Bataclan killers really Muslims?'

'Not if you ask the overwhelming majority of Muslims. Most Muslims consider them to be ignorant criminals who use Islam as a cover to carry out their vile crimes. But it makes very little difference. As far as most people are concerned, they were Muslims, full stop.'

'Yes, but the reason they did what they did was to punish the people who'd published those cartoons of Muhammad. They made it quite clear that the Prophet had been insulted and it was their job to avenge the Prophet by killing the cartoonists.'

'Those drawings weren't meant to be taken seriously. For me and for any true Muslim, the Prophet simply can't be caricatured. The Prophet is a spirit, a superior being that can never be captured with a few strokes of the pencil. It's also true that not everyone has the same view. But we all have the right to poke fun at what others consider to be sacred. It's part of the spirit of democracy and of freedom. The whole business should have been greeted with indifference. Frankly, when you see the drawings, do they really make you think of the Prophet? Like I said, *Charlie Hebdo* has ridiculed Christ many times, along with all the popes and plenty of rabbis. But no Catholic or Jew has ever thought to try and assassinate the cartoonist. And then, as I've said, many times, France is a country in which freedom of conscience and freedom of expression are sacred. Censorship no longer exists. If you're French, you have to accept these laws. If you are a French Muslim, you have to respect the laws of the Republic. That's what it means to be a citizen. But the Kouachi brothers and their accomplice Coulibaly acted in the name of a form of Islam that's propagated by international terrorism, whether it calls itself Al-Qaeda or Daesh.'

'But you see, what makes me afraid as a French girl of Muslim background, it's that people can be killed for blasphemy here in France even though this is a secular country and it's perfectly within our right to criticise religion.'

'Yes, and that right was hard-won. People battled for decades in France before the law was passed separating church and state. Every citizen has the right to believe in God or not. That's what it means to have freedom of conscience. It's up to us what our opinions are. You're free to make fun of religion and you won't be thrown into prison. Officially, secularism is defined as "the separation of civil society and religious society; the state has no religious powers and the churches have no political power".'

'Secularism is freedom.'

'Yes, but as I said, it was a long struggle before it was enshrined in law, especially the battle to keep religion out of public education. There are other European countries in which no such law has ever been passed – Spain or Italy, for example.'

'And I imagine no Arab country has such a law, either.'

'In Arab countries, the clan, the tribe, the family are considered more important than the individual. When you are born a Muslim, you are part of the "house of Islam" and you don't have the right to leave it. To leave the House means to become an apostate, a sort of outlaw, someone who has denied their roots and their allegiance. And as I've said, an apostate is considered to be a traitor, someone who must be punished by death.'

'What do you think the Islamist fanatics are most afraid of?'

'Freedom of expression is what they fear most, freedom of conscience, the freedom to doubt, to choose whether or not to believe. A freedom that is sacred in France. But it's quite clear that some Muslims in France don't accept it. Maybe that's why they don't integrate – because they can't accept that fundamental freedom.

'But to get back to the cartoons: let me tell you what a professor of theology from the University of Al-Azhar in Cairo had to say about them. Ashraf Adli was quoted in *Le Figaro* on 15 January 2015 and said this about the *Charlie Hebdo* team: "Those men were asking for trouble. I don't condone the attacks on them, but Muhammad is sacred for us, off-limits. If they are shot at again, they shouldn't complain." To which one of his colleagues added: "The more insulting drawings there are, the more extremist reactions there will be." The Grand Mufti of Jerusalem also denounced the "insult" that had "hurt the feelings of more than a billion Muslims around the world".'

'I see what you're saying. So are there actually any secular Arab or Muslim countries? It doesn't seem like there would be.'

'Only Turkey. It's the only officially secular state, since Mustafa Kemal came to power in 1924. But Erdogan, Turkey's current president, is leaning more and more towards Islamism. Apart from Turkey, there isn't a single country in the Muslim world, from North Africa, Africa, Asia to the Middle East that is secular. It's impossible even to discuss secularism. The problem is occasionally brought up by intellectuals, in Egypt, Morocco or Tunisia, but they are very much in the minority. And without secularism, there's no criticism, no room for doubt, no challenging of ideas. Islam is sacrosanct, never to be touched. It shows you how vulnerable Muslims feel, in every part of the world.'

'The other day, you said that Tunisia had taken a big step and voted in an extraordinary constitution. What was that all about?'

'Well, it began with the revolution of 2010–2011, after which the Tunisian parliament voted in a new constitution granting freedom of conscience and equal rights to men and women. It is the only such constitution in the Arab Muslim world, and it came about even with the presence of the Islamist Ennahda party in the parliament. So, yes, it's both revolutionary and unique, although it has to be said that the groundwork for the granting of these rights had been laid by the former president Habib Bourguiba (1903–2000). He'd already brought in a Family Law Code that gave the same rights to women and men. Of course, there were fundamentalists who tried to alter the code but they didn't succeed even after the murder of some who didn't agree with them. Since then, Tunisia has suffered a series of terrorist attacks: in March 2015, twenty-two people were killed in the Bardo National Museum, and in June of the same year a lone gunman killed thirty-eight people, mostly British tourists on a beach near Sousse. In November 2015 a bus carrying presidential guards on a main road in Tunis was bombed, and in March 2016 there was a large-scale attack against the army and police in Ben Guerdane, near the border with Libya, when forty-five people were killed, including twenty-eight of the attackers. So the terrorists, who claimed to represent Daesh, not only killed their fellow human beings, but they also effectively stifled the economy of this small country.'

'Why haven't any other Arab or Muslim countries brought in a constitution like the Tunisian one?'

'Because they're afraid that people won't accept it. Changing people's attitudes is no easy matter, and it's hard to get people to accept modern ideas and alter their behaviour. Modernity means recognising individual freedoms, and most important of all, it gives women equal status in the social system. And as I said earlier, it's the clan, the family, the tribe that come first in Arab Muslim societies, not the individual. Which may account for the lack of social progress in Arab Muslim societies. People at all levels of society cling to Islam; it's the one thing they all have in common. Islam provides a moral code, an identity to seek refuge in, a culture.'

'And what about Morocco? Has there been any change there?'

'They came close to including freedom of conscience in the new Constitution of 2011, but the Islamist Justice and Development Party campaigned relentlessly against it. And ever since they've been in power, they've worked to limit the exercise of freedom by doing things like censoring newspapers and films, foreign ones in particular.'

'Since the massacres of 7 and 9 January and then 13 November 2015, have non-fanatical Muslims protested in support of freedom?'

'Yes, on 11 January 2015, a group of sixty-seven intellectuals, artists, writers and academics from the Muslim world published an appeal stating:

'"The world is going through a war started by individuals and groups who claim to be from Islam. In Syria, Iraq, Libya, Tunisia, Nigeria, France etc., this war is the same. It is conducted in the name of a certain reading of Islam.

'"Reforms are needed in the Muslim world to counter this war. Citizenship, equality, freedom of conscience, the rule of law and human rights are indispensable antidotes.

'"Today, the answer to this war is not to say that Islam is not that. For it is in the name of a certain reading of Islam that these acts are committed. No, the answer is to recognise and affirm the historicity and inapplicability of a number of texts in the Muslim tradition. And to draw the conclusions."

'There you are. You'll say there are only sixty-seven signatures. But the petition exists and many more people will sign it. And in Morocco, after the Bataclan attacks, members of the ulema, Morocco's highest body of religious scholars, published a fatwa (in the sense of an advisory opinion) denouncing the attacks and roundly condemning this kind of terrorism, which serves only to sully Islam. This is not what Islam is. The king of Morocco, Mohammed VI, has also repudiated the terrorists: he gave a speech denouncing extremism and radicalism. He also called for anything that encourages intolerance and fanaticism to be removed from school textbooks. But in spite of all this, most people still hold Islam responsible, however much Muslims speak out against criminal Islamism. It's very difficult to reverse this trend.'

'So, if all this is true, do you think it's possible to be a practising Muslim in a secular democracy like France?'

'You can't change the dogma of Islamic faith. It is what it is. But Muslims can adapt their religious practices and adjust them according to the society they live in. When Islam is understood in an intelligent fashion, of course it's compatible with democracy. But Muslims have to respect the laws of the Republic. It's very important that they put the law of the land above their religion. Attempts have been made to define the terms of an Islam that is peaceful and calm, that respects the law of the land and is lived in private. But there's still a long way to go. For example, a man should not refuse to let his wife be examined by a male doctor when she needs medical attention. Nor should parents forbid their daughters to do PE at school because they consider the outfits worn to be too revealing. And it's not acceptable for people to demand single-sex swimming facilities or to cause disruption by stopping to pray in the street.'

'Yes, but what do you think? Can Islam be reformed? Will the petition make any difference?'

'Sooner or later all religions have to resolve this question. These days, it's Islam that's resisting it. And yet, when you read the texts written at the time of the Prophet, or during the Islamic Enlightenment from the ninth to the eleventh centuries, you say to yourself there's no reason at all why Islam shouldn't return to a golden age. Back then, Islam was characterised by intelligence and clear thinking, but nowadays the forces of regression are at work. They obstruct all attempts to debate these crucial questions. I'll give you an example. There was a reformist movement in Egypt in the nineteenth century. A man named Muhammad Abduh (1849–1905) worked with another reformist, a theologian of liberation named Jamal al-Din al-Afghani (1838–97). They were both rationalists who tried to free the scriptures from the fetters of tradition and dogma. They used to say that when there is a conflict between reason and tradition, reason should always prevail. They prized freedom and responsibility above all else and saw religion as a framework, within which people should strive to interpret texts in an intelligent, responsible manner, in keeping with the historical context of their day. Averroes, the great twelfth-century philosopher, said more or less the same thing: "The human spirit can find religious truth through reason." Basically, all of these thinkers based their ideas on three core principles: that people should be courageous in their thinking, that they should see things for what they are, and that freedom of thought could be achieved by fighting against prejudice and only bowing down to the truth.

'A Syrian man named Rashid Rida (1865–1935) was another thinker who was initially inspired by these rationalists. However, when he went to live in Saudi Arabia, he was influenced by the purist, hardline interpretation of Islam advocated by Muhammad Ibn Abd al-Wahhab. As you know, Wahhabism demanded strict application of the sharia, and this is the form of Islam that's dominant today in Saudi Arabia and most of the Gulf nations. It's also the philosophy followed by the Taliban, who could well be in power again in Afghanistan before long.

'Then there's Nasr Hamid Abu Zayd (1943–2010), the Egyptian writer who published a book in the 1990s suggesting a critical reading of the Qur'an. The result of that was that he was dismissed by the university and declared "apostate" by religious scholars. In other words, he was expelled from the "house of Islam", and designated as a target to be fought against and even killed. And because an apostate cannot be married to a Muslim, he was forced to separate from his wife, who had no choice but to divorce him: otherwise, she'd have been considered his accomplice and therefore also an "apostate". They eventually managed to flee to the Netherlands, where he died of ill-health, but also of rage and sorrow.'

'Has it always been like this? Or has Islam only recently become so intolerant?'

'It's not exactly new. But intolerance and sectarianism have certainly been intensifying since around the time of the Iranian Revolution in 1979. That was when Islam started to renew its dormant political ambitions. Ayatollah Khomeini, the leader of the Iranian Revolution, stated when he came to power: "Islam is political or it is nothing." But you have to go back a long way in the history of Islam to find other examples of such intransigence. In the thirteenth century, a scholar by the name of Ibn Taymiyyah (1263–1328) suggested a literal, word-for-word reading of the Qur'an. He came from Turkey, but went to live in Syria with his family after the Mongol invasion. I'll give you some examples of his harsh intolerance that might remind you of recent events. In 1293 he called for the death of a Christian accused of insulting the Prophet Muhammad, and continued his campaign even when the judges refused to agree with him. He waged a vicious campaign against the Sufi poets, people like Ibn Arabi (born in Murcia in 1165, died in Damascus 1240). And he was radically opposed to the Shias and fought relentlessly against them. And this was the theologian who inspired Muhammad Ibn Abd al-Wahhab, the man who later imposed Wahhabism, the most rigid form of Islam, in Arabia, putting into practice a literal interpretation of sharia and destroying mausoleums, statues and so on, whatever their historical significance. It's said that in 1744, Abd al-Wahhab and the emir, Ibn Saud, swore allegiance to the goal of ensuring the victory of the new doctrine by any means possible, including jihad.

'So you see, jihad has a long history; it would be a mistake to believe it was invented by Daesh.'

'But about Daesh, do they have a leader, a boss, who makes all the decisions?'

'We've known, since al-Baghdadi declared himself the caliph and made it clear that he intended to spread the so-called "Islamic State" all over the world, that a well-organised group exists, a group that makes extensive use of social networks to communicate. We know that there are military officers fighting under al-Baghdadi, most of whom were once members of Saddam Hussein's army, which the Americans disbanded when they invaded Iraq and ousted Saddam. The money for this "Islamic State" or Daesh ("Islamic State" in Syria and Iraq) has come from both states and private individuals. Saudi Arabia and Qatar have refused to acknowledge providing funds for these fighters, but it is well established that at the very least they allowed private organisations to send money to Daesh. And when Daesh fighters invaded Iraq, they emptied all the banks and started selling oil on the black market. Which means that they are wealthy and very well armed. These people are not amateurs.'

'What exactly do they want?'

'Their ideas come from Abou Moussab al-Souri. He was the one who thought up the "Islamic State" and devised the strategies aimed at recruiting young European Muslims and converts from other backgrounds. By the end of 2015 there were 15,000 jihadist fighters in Syria and Iraq. These fighters were given training and sent into battle, or in the case of some who either weren't cut out for battle or were reliable cadres, were sent back to their home countries to form "sleeper cells", ready to go into action when the order came to carry out an attack. These people aren't simply mercenaries being paid to fight: they're willing soldiers, silently fighting for a cause they believe will lead them to paradise. They're sometimes thought of as loners when in fact they are often family men, leading a normal life. To quote one of the Daesh propagandists: "To be worthy of the title of martyr, you must have something to lose: a son, a wife, a mother . . ." In other words, dying for jihad must come at a cost, the jihadist must pay a price. Otherwise their death would simply be suicide.'

'But Dad, that's so twisted! And this whole war is being fought in the name of Islam! How on earth can you expect people not to be afraid?'

'Of course people are afraid. We're all afraid. These people are fanatics, fighters who see no difference between slitting a lamb's throat for Eid, and slitting the throat of a human being they've taken hostage. People are right to be afraid. But how can you explain to them that this is not what Islam is?'

'I try to explain it to people, too. I tell them it's not Islam, but I can see they don't believe me.'

'Islam has become the West's new enemy. Ever since the Iranian Revolution in 1979 and the Soviet invasion of Afghanistan that same year. And most of all since the 9/11 attacks in New York. Before, in the days of the Cold War, the Soviet Union and communism were America's enemy. And then after the Berlin Wall came down in 1989 and the Soviet Union collapsed immediately afterwards, it's almost as if the Americans started looking for a new enemy to focus attention on. And now, thanks to Al-Qaeda and Daesh and the spectacular nature of their outrages, Islam, both as a religion and a culture, is being held responsible for a so-called "clash of civilisations".

'Cruelty, barbaric acts, regressive thinking, these are the things that have come to represent Islam. And yes, it is difficult to separate Islam from those images of murder in their videos, of barbarians cutting the throat of a Western hostage, or of a man burned alive, as that unfortunate Jordanian pilot was. Islam and its true values are polluted by all this. If ever Muslim countries needed to mobilise, now is the time. They need to denounce these savage acts. In May 2016, the president of the Tunisian Islamist Ennahda party Rached Ghannouchi did stand up and say: "Religious practice must be completely independent of political action." He also said: "Islam must no longer be hostage to politics." Which is the opposite of what Khomeini declared in 1979.'

'I don't think it's enough just to condemn it. Something needs to actually be done...'

'But Western countries are guilty of hypocrisy on this. They know that strict Wahhabism is enforced in Saudi Arabia, and they also know that Wahhabism is the dogma Daesh has vowed to enforce in its territories. In Saudi Arabia, women have virtually no rights – only since December 2015 have Saudi women been able to vote. Now they even have the right to be elected, and to drive. And yet, when it comes to doing business, Europeans close their eyes to these shocking aspects.'

'Muslim immigrants have been coming to Europe for decades – there are millions of Muslims in Europe now. How is it possible for us all to live side by side?'

'There's no problem with people who've lived in Europe for a long time: they work, pay their taxes and discreetly get on with their lives. That doesn't mean they're not shocked, though, when a magazine publishes caricatures of the Prophet. The Prophet is sacred for them. A believer simply can't accept the idea of caricaturing the Prophet. It's an assault on their most cherished ideal. You can't ask them to approve of the ridiculing of the one they worship and celebrate, the one the Qur'an describes as the "best of all creatures" (*Khayr al-An'âm*).'

'So what is the problem then?'

'It seems to be with the second and even the third generation, among the children and grandchildren of immigrants: people who were born in Europe and have European passports. Many of them have been brought up in a cultural vacuum, with parents who couldn't cope and lost control of their children. The unhealthy, toxic environment of the *banlieues* hasn't helped either. Unemployment in the immigrant suburbs is often as much as 45%, while the national average is more like 10%. It's desperately sad. Some youngsters in the *banlieues* don't really feel French. They turn to other things, and in Islam, they find an answer to their troubles, they feel reassured. But most of all, Islam gives them an identity. Their road to jihad often starts with petty crime, followed by a spell in prison, where they fall under the influence of indoctrinators who lure them with images of a glittering future in the battle against the West that has despised and neglected them so, where women have abandoned all modesty and men marry other men. So some young people come out of prison willing to go into battle against the "infidels". Their numbers may not be vast, but there are enough of them to keep the networks of fighters in Syria and Iraq well supplied.'

'Dad, I'll ask you again: is Islam really compatible with democracy and secularism? I'm not talking about radical Islam, fundamentalism or any of those murderous offshoots. I mean Islam as you describe it, the healthy, sane form of Islam.'

'Of course it's compatible, precisely because there are more Muslims than ever living peacefully and in perfect harmony with other communities in France...'

# Muhammad

The figure of The Prophet Muhammad occupies a central position in Islam. Muslims' attachment to God's messenger is held sacred. The entire Muslim community considers Muhammad to be 'the first light created by God'. Furthermore, God 'sent' Muhammad to all of humanity. Verse 28 of Surah 34 says: 'We have not sent you but to all of humanity.' Elsewhere, the Prophet is speaking and says: 'Say: Oh, mankind, I am God's messenger to you all' (verse 158, Surah 7). And according to Ali, Muhammad's son-in-law, the Prophet said: 'I was a light before my Master, 14,000 years before He created Adam.'

As the last Messenger of God, Muhammad is the 'Seal of the Prophets'. The line of prophecies ends with him. He is therefore a spiritual entity that is both sovereign and eternal. No one can claim to be a prophet after him. He is God's elect, the embodiment of spiritual heritage. In Surah 3, verse 81, God says: 'I give you a Book, and wisdom; after me will come a messenger, one who is sent to confirm what you have received; believe in him therefore and give him assistance.'

For all these reasons, this higher Spirit, which is both eternal and universal, cannot be likened to the image depicted in those infamous cartoons. In no way do these cartoons represent the 'Spirit', which exists fundamentally beyond our reach.'

'Stop right there, Dad! Do you really think that things are fine between Muslims and other communities?'

'Jihadists are only a very small minority, they don't represent the community of Muslims in France at all. Muslims here are a diverse community, you can't lump them all together. But the activities of jihadists are constantly in the news and I can see how people might get the impression that all Muslims, even the most peaceable of them, are somehow involved. A poll conducted in April 2016 suggested that 47% of French people and 43% of Germans considered Muslims to be a threat. Islam's image all over Europe is getting worse and worse.'

'So what's the cause of the problem?'

'Some of the kids are angry and the people at the top of Daesh, the ones bent on establishing "Islamic State" all over the world, take advantage of that anger. They do everything they can to widen the gulf between young Muslims and the rest of French society. They fill young people's heads with ideas about the West; they say it's sinful, that it's turned away from spiritual and religious values. Or they make them believe their true lives lie elsewhere, in the "brotherhood of Muslims", in the "house of Islam", in the virtue of sacrificing themselves to be "worthy of paradise". That's how they often manage to detach people from the West and turn them against it.'

'But what does all that have to do with Morocco? There are more than 2,500 Moroccans in Daesh, too, and Morocco's a Muslim country! So why do all these young Moroccans sign up for Daesh?'

'Some people in Morocco, and in other Muslim countries like Algeria, Tunisia and Egypt, think there should be an "Islamic State" all over the world, a state founded on the principles of Wahhabism, in other words, along the strictest of lines. And they think Daesh can do that. The progressive political parties in these countries haven't managed to get through to these people.'

'All the same, Dad, I often hear people say that Islam and democracy are incompatible. So I ask you again: isn't there some truth to that?'

'If we can manage to demonstrate that it's perfectly possible to be a practising Muslim and live in harmony with other people, then yes, you can certainly say that Islam is compatible with democracy. But it's hard for Muslims to accept the idea of secularism. Islam is all-encompassing: it provides the believer with a religion, a moral code, a vision of the world, a daily routine. It's difficult for a believer to spontaneously imagine that a Muslim country could separate mosque and state. And in fact, as you know, Turkey is the only Muslim country that has ever attempted to be secular. Who knows, maybe Tunisia will succeed one day.'

'So what you're saying is that it's not easy?'

'I have to admit, that as long as the radicals continue to stir up unrest in Muslim areas, it seems to me that Islam will be in great difficulties in European countries.'

'Dad, some people in France wonder what mistakes the West has made with regard to Muslims.' What has it done wrong? What do you think?'

'The mistakes were made a long time ago in the colonial period. Wrongs were done and memories in places like France and Algeria are still bruised. The wounds are still open. There's been too much violence, too much hatred, too much humiliation. Relations haven't healed. France encouraged the waves of immigration that followed independence, but there's been more immigration since then that wasn't so welcome. And Muslim immigrants from North Africa or sub-Saharan Africa haven't exactly found paradise in France. It's well known that immigrants from France's former colonies have had to endure a great deal of suffering and misunderstanding.

'There used to be scholars in the West known as Orientalists, academics who were specialists in Islam and the Arab world. They studied the Islamic world with intelligence and good will and showed great empathy. Today the tradition is carried on by Gilles Kepel, Henry Laurens and Olivier Roy, to name a few of them. These are people who know their subjects well and make thoughtful contributions. But now there are also these journalists who claim to be experts and discuss the issues without really understanding them. Some of them are very good observers but the Orientalists had, and still have, a much greater depth of knowledge.'

'What exactly do you mean when you say that France wasn't very welcoming to its immigrants?'

'Immigrants have been stigmatised and blamed for all sorts of things. There was a major oil crisis in 1973 and immigrants in France, especially if they were from North Africa, were singled out and held responsible for the increase in the price of oil. Violence erupted and there were a number of racist attacks and crimes that were racially motivated, particularly in the area in and around Marseille where North African immigration was concentrated.'

'And the immigrants themselves hadn't committed any attacks against French people, had they?'

'No, absolutely not. And to make matters worse, governments of right and left alike have not done enough to improve the living conditions of immigrants and their French-born children. Immigrant support agencies have warned the authorities again and again of the need to pay attention to immigrant communities. After the Iranian Revolution in 1979, some imams in French mosques began urging people to scrupulously respect the teachings of Islam, indoctrinating young immigrants and asking women to wear the veil. Around the same time, Muslim prisoners of North African origin began demanding halal meals, as a way of proclaiming their identity. And in the 1980s the demand for halal meat went beyond the prisons and became more widespread. It took some time for this form of Islamism, which eventually gave rise to terrorism, to become established in immigrant communities in France, just as it did in Belgium in places like Molenbeek in Brussels. And Molenbeek is now considered to be a main haunt of terrorists of North African origin.'

'How do you explain the fact that Islamism took hold so easily in these districts?'

'There's a fairly simple explanation. Young people who have no prospects are discontented, culturally, socially and politically. They have nothing to cling on to, nowhere to focus their ambitions. Islam is presented to them in such a way as to give them ready-made answers to their existential questions. And then there's the propaganda on the internet and social media, perfect platforms for indoctrination. It's not hard to see why a young person with no future, living in a *banlieue* cut off from society, might succumb to the attractions of a video of jihadists talking about how they've found a meaning for their lives.'

'But isn't there a risk of blaming Europeans and Americans for everything? Shouldn't Muslims recognise where they've gone wrong, too?'

'Well, yes, they should. But you have to take into account the historical background. It's not a question of laying the blame on others, but simply a way of putting it all into its historical context. We haven't even mentioned the Crusades, nine of them altogether, from Pope Urban II's call to Christians to go to war against Muslims in 1095 to the future King Edward I of England's war against Muslims in 1271–72. I've already described how, in Europe, there were wars between Catholics and Protestants. Thousands of Protestants were massacred in France on St. Bartholomew's Day, 24 August 1572, during the Wars of Religion. So to put it all in context, you always have to keep in mind what terrible violence was done in Europe in the name of Christianity.'

'Okay, fine. But I still don't see how France could be considered responsible for what's happening now.'

'Well, quite apart from the absence of policies aimed at improving conditions for immigrant communities in the *banlieues*, there's the question of Israel and what many Muslims see as the double standard in Western attitudes. Rightly or wrongly, immigrants and their French-born children get very angry when they see European countries defending the State of Israel and forgetting the injustices done to Palestinians. People were very upset when President Hollande spoke of "Israel's right to defend itself" on the first day of the Gaza War in July 2014. And then Prime Minister Manuel Valls joined in and proclaimed his "unwavering support" for Israel and declared that any criticism of Zionism was "disguised anti-Semitism". Valls seemed to have forgotten that in 2006 when he was Mayor of Évry, he'd spoken of his support for the Palestinian people's struggle, in the presence of Leïla Shahid, the ambassador of the Palestinian Authority in France at the time. And now there was not a word of compassion for the Palestinians, no mention of Palestinian civilian losses. Hollande did later publish a more balanced statement but the original declaration was circulated widely on social networks. It's a bad memory for the Muslim community in France. You only have to look at the videos on YouTube of Muslims protesting vehemently against what was said.'

'And since then, have the French changed their policy towards the Middle East?'

'No, they haven't. In January 2016, at the commemoration of the 2015 attacks, Manuel Valls condemned anti-Semitism and restated his support for the State of Israel. He said he could not accept what he called "compulsive hatred for the State of Israel". But there was no mention of the increase in Islamophobic acts in France nor of the ongoing colonisation of the occupied territories. He restated his position several weeks later, on 7 March 2016, at a dinner with the CRIF (Representative Council of French Jewish Institutions) when he said: "Anti-Zionism is synonymous with anti-Semitism and with hatred of Israel."'

'And what about President Hollande? Did he say anything else?'

'He made a symbolic gesture on 10 January 2016 and went to have tea in the Great Mosque of Paris. It was an important thing to do, but in the eyes of the Muslim population, it wasn't enough.'

'But even so, it's hardly enough to incite terrorism.'

'No, and it absolutely does not justify Merah, the Kouachis and Coulibaly murdering cartoonists and

Jewish children in the name of Islam, or in Merah's case, in the name of Palestine. Merah was the one who killed Jewish schoolchildren in Montauban. He claimed he did it because "the Jews have killed our brothers and sisters in Palestine". No, Palestinians were shocked by those terrible crimes; people in Ramallah and Gaza don't want these individuals claiming to represent their cause.'

'Would you say that Muslims are guilty of racism, too? Or are they merely victims of other people's racism?'

'Racism is a scourge that afflicts all of humanity. Why would you expect Muslims to escape it? Of course there are Muslims who are racists: there are plenty of Muslims who don't like mixing with people who are strangers to their culture any more than Western racists do. Nor do they tolerate agnostics, atheists, people with no religion, or simply people who practise a different religion. Suspicion and mistrust exist everywhere. Just because you're a victim of racism doesn't mean you're immune to being racist.'

'The number of Muslims in the world is growing: they say there are currently more than 1.3 billion Muslims. Does that make you think the future belongs to Islam?'

'It's undeniable that religions play a very important role in the modern world and this century has certainly been dominated by issues around Islam. Daesh has declared war on the whole world in the name of Islam. Christianity in the form of

Catholicism is on the wane. But still, I just can't believe that the future is in the hands of any one religion.'

'When do you think we'll see an end to Islamophobia?'

'Fear of Islam is real, we've already talked about that. That fear is often blind and simplistic. People start to hate all immigrants, even though most immigrants would never want to quarrel with anyone. And then of course there are the Muslim men who impose a strict code on their wives and daughters, insisting that they wear the veil and cover themselves completely, including their faces – covering your face in public is illegal now in France. (Incidentally, it's not only Muslim women who cover their faces: in Yemen, for example, women were wearing the veil before the arrival of Islam.) They won't let their womenfolk go to places where both sexes mingle, or allow them to be examined by male doctors. But these things are absurd, they're not really to do with Islam. Although people aren't likely to be convinced of that any time soon...'

'Actually, it's all to do with women, isn't it?'

'Yes. Most of the tension in the Muslim world today has to do with the way women are treated. You're absolutely right: it's all centred on the female body. Basically, it's a problem of unresolved sexuality. The female body is the focus of all anxiety. That's why Islamist purists insist on women being covered up. It's not just that the body can't be shown, its freedom must be restricted, too; it can't be allowed to move freely, to be fully alive. Westerners are shocked by these regressive practices, as are open-minded Muslims. But most of the responsibility for the rise in Islamophobia lies with Osama bin Laden and his successors Daesh and its army of mercenaries. There was an article in *Le Figaro* recently on this very topic, an interview with Henry Laurens, the Professor of Modern History of the Arab and Muslim World at the Collège de France on 15 January 2015. In it, he said: "I think Islamophobia is primarily caused by those Muslims who incite people to hate. Unlike traditional anti-Semitism, Islamophobia is largely a reaction to a way of behaving, to particular actions. I prefer not to use the term 'racism', which draws on biology, when the very idea of the existence of races is in itself questionable. I prefer to use the Anglo-Saxon term 'hate crime.'"

'How can we stop these hate crimes?'

'First of all, Muslims have to make some changes to the way they live in the West. Education and culture are essential if we are to combat the image of Islam that inspires fear. The Qur'an is full of poetry, it's humane and beautiful. But it has to be read with intelligence. If you interpret it narrowly and apply what it says literally, you can make it mean all kinds of things.

'And the West, too, must be more open and try to understand Islam in greater depth. Instead of focusing on violent acts that perpetuate the idea of a war between two opposing visions of the world, the West should get to know the culture and civilisation of the Islamic world. Yes, the best way to combat Islamophobia is to fight against ignorance on all sides.'

# The next day...

'Dad, what's that book you're reading?'

'The Qur'an.'

'But haven't you already read it, several times?'

'Yes, but it's a very rich book and it needs to be read many times.'

'Isn't that the book you learnt by heart when you were little?'

'Yes, it is. Like all the kids of my generation, I was sent to the Qur'anic school in the mosque in our neighbourhood. An old man made us recite it all, verse by verse.'

'And do you still remember it?'

'Yes, it's still all there. But when I learnt it, I didn't understand it. I memorised whole surahs, that is chapters, and I didn't know what any of it meant. The old man didn't explain the Qur'an to us; his job was merely to make us learn the verses by heart.'

'And you really did learn them all?'

'I had to! I was terrified. I was so scared, I made sure I memorised everything.'

'And if you didn't learn it?'

'We were beaten on the soles of our feet, with a stick. It wasn't funny at all.'

'No, but I can't help laughing at the thought of you with your feet up in the air.'

'Yes, well I did commit the whole of the Qur'an to memory.'

'So why are you reading it again now?'

'Because there are several different ways you can read it; I'm trying out a new method at the moment.'

'What do you mean?'

'Well, it's like this. The Qur'an is the Muslims' holy book. Every religion has sacred books to which it refers: for Christians, it's the Bible; and for Jews, the Torah. But these three books have much in common. Their appeal has to be universal and timeless. So you have to know how to approach them, how to read them. You need to learn how to read these texts intelligently.'

'So what's this new method you're using?'

'I'll give you a bit of a history lesson so you'll understand what I'm talking about. As you know, the Qur'an is made up of a collection of messages from Allah, sent to the Prophet Muhammad through the angel Gabriel. Muhammad was chosen by God to be His messenger to the Arab tribes, who at that time worshipped stone idols. Muhammad received the messages in the year 622 of the Christian era.'

'Yes, but what does that have to do with the different ways of reading the Qur'an?'

'Well, at the time, some people interpreted those messages metaphorically. They saw them as symbols.'

'Sorry to keep stopping you, but what does metaphorical mean?'

'A metaphor is an image the helps us understand hidden meanings.'

'Give me an example.'

'Well, here's a riddle: which animal walks on four legs in the morning, stands on two at noon and walks on three in the evening?'

'I don't know. I give in.'

'The answer is man! If you think of a man's lifespan as one whole day, the morning is the equivalent of infancy, noon is adulthood and evening is old age, when the man walks with a cane. That's a metaphor, a form of comparison that describes things with pictures to make them easier to understand.'

'Okay, I get it.'

'So, to come back to reading the Qur'an. When I say it has to be read with intelligence, what I mean is you can't simply take the words at face value. You have to look for the "spirit" behind the words and phrases.'

'You have to be pretty clever to interpret metaphors.'

'No, you just have to understand that God speaks through symbols and images. Images that aren't based on concrete reality.'

'What do you mean?'

'I mean they don't come from the real world: when you take a photograph, you're taking a picture of the real world as it appears to us. But if I say this man has lost his head, I don't mean he's had his head chopped off, what I'm saying is that he's gone mad. That's another example of a metaphor. And when God speaks of people who don't believe in Him, He says: "They have strayed": they've lost their way, they're on the wrong path. In the same way, when He speaks of the "hand of God", He's not talking about a flesh and blood hand, He's using an image that in fact depicts quite the opposite: a spirit, something that is not material.'

'Okay.'

'We talked yesterday about the disagreements throughout history between those who read the Qur'an literally, word for word, and those who used their powers of reason to understand the spirit of the words: those who were unwilling to read between the lines, and those who were ready to use their own intelligence and ability to think freely in order to understand God's words. It's the same today: there are the fanatics who refuse all discussion and won't accept any form of disagreement, and then there are the people who want to discuss the ideas in the Qur'an, who believe we should use our minds and think for ourselves. And those are the people the fanatics persecute and brand as infidels.'

'Okay, I know, you've already talked about fundamentalism and about the people whose interpretation of the word of God is rigid and narrow. But why would anyone put words into the Qur'an that aren't there and twist what it says?'

'When the Prophet Muhammad died on 8 June 632, he left no instructions about the verses the angel

Gabriel had imparted to him. His companions knew those verses by heart and some of them wrote them down. But the Qur'an as an entity, a single document, or *Mushaf* as it's called, didn't exist at that point. That didn't happen until more than twenty years later when Uthman, the third Caliph of Islam, brought together a committee of six specially chosen companions and charged them with compiling a single definitive text.'

'So for twenty years or so, there was no such thing as the Qur'an?'

'The Qur'an existed, but only in people's memories and hearts, not in the form of an actual book. And when it was all written down, the surahs, or chapters of the Qur'an, were written without any vowels. It wasn't until two hundred years later that a "vowelled" version became available. And from that moment onwards, the two world views came into conflict through different readings of the Qur'an. The first group were the theologians of the Mu'tazilite tradition, rationalists who read the text symbolically and metaphorically and used their power of reason to interpret it. The Qur'an for them was something that had a definite beginning – it hadn't always existed. God is eternal, but the Qur'an had actually been created. They believed that the will of God is rational and fair, and that it's possible for people to understand and act in accordance with it. There were other philosophers, too, people like al-Kindi, al-Farabi, Avicenna and Averroes, who believed that the world we live in should be understood for what it is, and not simply as a manifestation of God's divine power. Nowadays we'd call these thinkers modernists. They came into conflict with the traditionalists who believed the Qur'an should be read in a strictly literal fashion, with no room for interpretation or multiple readings. The traditionalists followed the teachings of Ibn Hanbal, a philosopher who rejected the notion of free will. He believed that everything was determined by God, that God was all-powerful, and that divine power was something humans would never be able to grasp.

'The traditionalist way of thinking continued to be promoted by other thinkers, in the fourteenth century by Ibn Tammiyyah, and then later in the eighteenth century by Muhammad Ibn Abd al-Wahhab. It gave rise to what we now call fundamentalism. We've already talked about Abd al-Wahhab – he was the Saudi scholar who turned Islam into the hard-line dogma that's practised today in Saudi Arabia and Qatar. Remember, we talked about the fact that Wahhabism relies on a very strict interpretation of sharia. It's a fanatical and backward-looking point of view; it's the complete opposite of the spirit of enlightenment that was so prevalent in the early centuries of Islam.'

'Yes, you've already explained all this. Go on.'

'I may be repeating myself, but I want to make sure you get the most important points. The traditionalist way of thinking says that the Qur'an exists outside of time and space; it's beyond the power of reason.

So, dogma wins out over reason, a dogma based on the word of God. And for the traditionalists, the word of God *is* God. But if you read the Qur'an carefully, instead of just memorising and repeating the verses, you see that what it suggests is quite the opposite. Many of the verses in the Qur'an arose in a specific context at a precise moment in history; they commented on situations that were unfolding at the time. Other verses, however, related to more than just that one time and place and so their relevance is for all time.

'Traditionalists find this provocative. They simply cannot tolerate the idea of reading the Qur'an in this way. It threatens their stock in trade of keeping the masses in ignorance. But what's at stake here is of fundamental importance. We're talking about breathing new life into the strain of humanism that runs through the Qur'an. And that's no small matter!

'Of course, it's usually ignorance that prevails. But that's no reason to give up. In his book *Understanding the Qur'an Today*, Mahmoud Hussein puts it like this: "By showing that Islam is both a divine message and a human story, by reintegrating the dimension of time, by finding the living truth of the Revelation beneath interpretations that fix it for all time, reformist thought is a school of freedom and responsibility. It gives every believer the opportunity to combine his faith in God with his worldly intelligence."'[9]

---

[9] *Understanding the Qur'an Today*, Saqi Books, 2013

'I'm going to ask you a simple question, Dad, but it's something I really need to understand. What exactly are the basic principles of Islam?'

'I don't need to refer to any books to answer that one. Basically you want to know what makes Islam, as the last of the revealed religions, a religion of peace and tolerance. After all, the word Islam itself comes from the same root as the Arabic word for peace.

'First of all, a Muslim must believe in a single all-powerful God. To become a Muslim, you have to declare that "there is no God but God and Muhammad is His prophet."

'Secondly, you must respect the "five pillars of Islam". In other words you must pray five times a day according to the position of the sun; you must abstain from food, drink and sexual relations between sunrise and sunset during the period of Ramadan (a month of twenty-nine or thirty days); you must give ten per cent of your earnings to charity, *Zakat*; and if you have the means and are in good health, you must make a pilgrimage to Mecca.

'These five pillars are the basics of Islam. Next, you must do no wrong. You must behave in a moral fashion, in accordance with basic humanitarian values: you must not steal, lie, betray, kill or take your own life (because it goes against divine will), nor commit evil. All religions teach these same values. And to that you must add loyalty, fraternity, piety and respect for spirituality.

'The Qur'an specifically condemns anyone who takes the life of an innocent person (Surah V, verse 32):

'"He who kills a man who has not himself committed murder, or who has done no violence on earth, is considered to have killed all men; and he who saves one single human life is considered to have saved all of humankind."'

# Two days later...

'Dad, to wrap things up, I'd like you to go over the steps you think we need to take now to successfully combat Islamist terrorism – like you did for the basic tenets of Islam. It was really clear and I found it easy to remember.'

'Well, we have to act over the long term. There is no miracle cure. But here, in my opinion, is what we need to do:

1. We need to focus on education. We should look carefully at school textbooks and make sure our teaching of the history of the three monotheistic religions is without bias. We should pay constant attention to teaching the values of tolerance, explaining the workings of racism and combatting fanaticism. In other words, we need an ambitious approach to teaching if we're to stop young people being lured into terrorism. Every subject in the curriculum should be infused with the same basic civic values, from the early years onwards and all the way through secondary school. Things won't change overnight, but it will yield results when today's children become adults.

2. We need to take a good look at what goes on in prisons. Imams should be trained and given the tools to enlighten young prisoners in order to prepare them for their return to society. Jihadist recruiters should be tracked down and prevented from doing further harm.
3. We need to examine what goes on in mosques. Imams should no longer be financed by foreign powers; no one should be able to simply proclaim themselves an imam; imams should be properly trained, they should be ready to promote peaceful values instead of merely proselytizing.
4. There needs to be a profound change in housing policy. Families should be involved and a serious effort should be made to get vulnerable young people from disadvantaged backgrounds into work.
5. The principles of secularism must be strictly enforced. No religion should ever be permitted to stray into the public domain. People need to fully understand exactly what secularism is. The responsibility for explaining the principles of secularism should lie with our educational system. The media should play a part in this, too.'

# And lastly...

'One last question, Dad: what should I be doing? What can I do, as a girl from a Muslim background, who's secular and both French and Moroccan, like you? How can I help to put a stop to terrorism?'

'You can carry on learning and calling things into question. Carry on with your studies and be vigilant, set an example as a person with values, the values of respect and tolerance. Be open and curious about other people at all times. Ultimately, only learning and knowledge can conquer the sickening ideology of terrorism, wherever it comes from. Read, listen to music, go to the theatre, learn languages, travel and always place knowledge above prejudice. And in a world in which many women are denied their rights, you must always stand up for your rights as a woman. You are fortunate to belong to two countries, two cultures. Make the most of it, make it an advantage. Terrorism will be defeated, perhaps through political struggle or even perhaps in armed combat, but always remember that the state must never, in any circumstances, abandon its values. We have to combat terrorism with laws and with justice, not with the weapons or methods of terrorism. It's true that when we see such barbarity we're at a loss what to do. As Voltaire put it in his *Treatise on Tolerance*: "How can I argue with the man who thinks he'll achieve salvation by cutting my throat?" The only arguments we have today are law and rigorous justice.'

'Yes, I know, education is usually the answer. But what about the people who are highly educated and still become terrorists?'

'In those cases, I have to admit it's probably more to do with psychology than politics. It could be to do with the unspoken, hidden things that go on in the unconscious mind, with things that are taboo. You can't always tell what's going on inside someone's head; appearances can be deceptive. The usual explanations don't work. What makes someone decide in absolute secrecy to change the course of their lives? Maybe they have some form of depression that's not obvious to other people, a bleak view of everyday life that makes them particularly sensitive to the hardships and injustices of the world, and that makes them susceptible to a radical change of direction. "I can't change the world, so I'll change myself and sign up to a cause." They look around and see no cause for hope and turn to something that's physically and mentally far removed from their lives.

'There are so many factors that can lead to this kind of sudden and unexpected transformation; let me try and identify a few of them, at least those that have to do with young Europeans from immigrant communities.

'It can often be to do with a complicated sense of frustration; when someone doesn't manage to find their place in society, or find any kind of fulfilment. Sometimes people are obsessed with the idea of status, with being someone, being known and recognised. Our society celebrates individual success, achievement, performance. We're surrounded by advertising, on billboards and on our television screens, on our phones and tablets, you can't get away from it. And it's aimed at the people who feel left out of this constant celebration of beauty, strength, success and machismo. Everything is to do with the individual in the West, where individual success is prized above all else.'

'Yes, it's true. We do celebrate the individual. But where most second-generation immigrants' parents come from, things are very different.'

'Yes, and if people feel they have no future, it's hard for them to go along with all this individualism. They experience one failure after another at school, they may come from a dysfunctional family in which there's no coming together to talk and support one another. Kids hang around in stairwells or on the street with older kids who may have found a means of making easy money and have lost their way.'

'And then what happens?'

'Family plays a big part. If you can't have a "normal" family, you create a family for yourself, become part of a "tribe". You're with your brothers, you're ready for adventure. Don't forget, the most recent attacks in France and Belgium were committed by brothers, the Kouachi, Coulibaly and Abdeslam brothers. (The Abdeslam brothers, Brahim and Salah, were among the perpetrators of the 13 November 2015 attacks in Paris.) And the two Chechens who planted bombs on the Boston marathon route on 15 April 2013 were brothers. The Tsarnaev brothers killed three and injured 264 people that day. And Mohammed Merah, who killed all those people in Toulouse and Montauban, was influenced by his older brother, Abdelkader Merah, who in turn used to hang around with Olivier Corel, a Syrian refugee living a quiet life in Artigat in south-west France.'

'Yes, but so what?'

'Brothers are less likely to betray one another, they're loyal. And family ties can lead people to take action sooner. You don't walk away from your brother, you don't turn your back on him. You're in it together, for better or worse. People need family ties, they crave those tribal bonds. And often there's a dominant male family member, exerting his power over his brothers and sisters. Families in many immigrants' countries of origin are patriarchal, they are dominated by a senior male figure. So the terror networks in Europe perpetuate the patriarchal family structure. Did you know there were six brothers among the 9/11 terrorists?'

'So you're saying that going into action alongside your brother is a way of rejecting European individualism?'

'Yes, it's a way of rebelling against the freedoms enjoyed by individuals in the West. And particularly the freedoms women have. A North African brought up to believe that men are superior, encouraged by his mother to believe this, finds the rights accorded to a woman in the West intolerable. He can't accept the freedom and autonomy that women have. Steeped in shame and hypocrisy, he can't accept the images of women's bodies around him. He fears that his sister or his wife will be contaminated by this freedom that strips men of their power over women.'

'Do you think parents are to blame?'

'Well, one of Mohammed Merah's brothers had broken off from his family. He said he had nothing in common with them, that he needed to "educate" his parents. There are mothers who put these kinds of ideas into their son's heads, but they do it because that's the tradition; they don't realise how much damage it can do in a society where these ideas aren't the norm. It's all so different from what they're used to.'

'And what do you have to say about the Moroccans and others living in North Africa, who aren't immigrants, and who still go off to Syria to wage jihad?'

'North African society is evolving. It's moving more towards the European way of life. When an Islamist sees a Moroccan woman claiming her rights, a Tunisian woman demanding her freedom or an

Algerian woman refusing to bow down to her older brother, it confirms all his worst fears. Islamists are everywhere in Morocco, complaining constantly about the spread of vice and corruption and the lack of "moral rigour" and respect for the precepts of Islam. They're convinced they were put on this Earth to re-establish virtue and morality and they do everything they can to influence domestic policy. Those who join the jihadists aren't necessarily involved in fighting an all-out war on the West, they're fighting Western influence in their own country where they no longer feel at home.'

'What kind of things do they do?'

'In Tunisia, the army and police are weak. Jihadists took advantage of that to murder German and British tourists; not only did they kill Westerners, but they undermined tourism at the same time.'

'Why?'

'They equate tourism with evil. Tourism brings a kind of liberation of customs, and the presence of foreigners can fuel an increase in demand for prostitution. Islamists believe they have to purge society of all they consider to be impure. They're obsessed with purification and fixated on desire and the female form. Jihadists are fanatical about women being covered up and insist that Muslim women must keep their bodies hidden and out of sight. It's an obsession with them.'

'Is there something wrong with these people?'

'That's not for me to say. It's up to the psychiatrists who examine them when they're arrested to decide things like that.'

'But what possible advantage can they get out of killing German or Italian tourists. How does that help their cause?'

'It doesn't! All terrorism does is spread terror; they want to make Europe tremble, it's as simple as that.'

'Why don't Arab countries come together to combat this terrorism? After all, it's ruining the image of Islam and the whole Arab world.'

'Arabs have never managed to unite, you know that. It's an old story. Look at the map of the Arab world; Algeria detests Morocco and tries to stir up trouble over the Western Sahara, which Morocco took back in 1974. And then look at Libya, in a state of chaos, with Daesh and its supporters taking advantage of that chaos. Egypt is ruled by a dictator who's thrown more than 40,000 dissenters into prison and made people "disappear" (which Human Rights Watch reported in detail in April 2016); Lebanon is still at war with Israel and now they have to cope with absorbing more than a million Syrian refugees. Jordan has to take in Syrian refugees, and cope with the threat of Daesh. As for Iraq, not a week goes by without a car bomb going off. And the situation in Syria, as you're well aware, is absolutely tragic: the number of civilian victims of the war was estimated by the UN in April 2016 to be more than 400,000, with several million refugees and people displaced.

And while Bashar al-Assad continues to slaughter his own people, radical Islamists he's freed from prison rejoin the ranks of Daesh and add to the destruction of Syria. It's no secret that Daesh was originally financed by people in Saudi Arabia and Qatar. And all this time, part of this same Arab world has been involved in a pointless war in Yemen, with the Saudis fighting against the Shia there. And that's what the whole mess really comes down to: the Gulf Arabs fear the power of Iran, where the vast majority of people are Shia. And Iran is far more structured, organised and determined than all the Arab states put together.'

'It's hopeless!'

'I know. There are so many Arab states, but there's no one unified Arab entity, no single strong, solid cohesive whole.'

'So terrorism will continue into the future?'

'Sadly, yes. Terrorism is a scourge with many complex ramifications. And we haven't seen the last of it.'

'Come on, Dad. Can't you end on a little note of hope?'

'Yes, I can. We can put all our efforts into education; we'll do everything in our power to make sure a new generation of young people emerges, young people who won't be duped into swallowing any old lies. Now more than ever, we have to support education, in schools, in families, in the media, on every platform and in every corner where there's a chance to repair the damage that's been done by so many lies and so much hate.'

# By way of an afterword

*Some thoughts on the loneliness of the intellectual of Muslim background, torn between the freedom of conscience he enjoys in France, and his place in the Ummah, the community of Islam, which does not allow him to exercise that freedom.*

Everything associated with Islam has taken a tragic turn. How is it that Islam is so fragile? One incident and fanatical, hysterical crowds take to the streets and burn flags and effigies of European chiefs of state.

'Calm down,' you want to say to them. 'It's only a drawing! And it's not the Prophet in that cartoon; the Prophet is a higher spirit, whose beauty and wit can't be reproduced. It's impossible to capture such a spirit on paper. So please, I beg you, don't demean the Prophet by reducing Him to such a platitude.'

Such words fall on deaf ears. The Ummah includes all Muslims, good and bad. You can't just walk away. You are born a Muslim and you die a Muslim. Leaving Islam means paying a high price. That road leads to apostasy. And God punishes the apostate, but not here on Earth, although that doesn't stop some states from carrying out the death sentence or subjecting people to public ignominy. Saudi Arabia, in particular.

Crowds are inherently deaf and blind.

One day, as I came to the end of a lecture I was giving at the University of Fez, a student stood up and asked me a question point-blank: 'Do you believe in God?'

After a short silence, I replied: 'Your question is indiscreet. I am under no obligation to give you an answer.'

Muttering started up in the lecture hall. I realised I was standing before an ad hoc tribunal.

So I began to talk to these students about the principle of freedom of conscience, of the right to keep one's beliefs private, of the freedom to choose how to live one's life and what to keep to oneself.

I was wasting my breath. My words came up against a series of brick walls. They could not be countenanced, could not even be heard.

Someone shouted: 'You're an atheist. You don't have the courage to admit it!'

'I won't be dragged into that trap,' I replied. 'I insist on my right to keep my beliefs to myself and not share them with anyone.'

Shouting and whistling from the audience. I was done for. The dean ushered me out through a hidden door and made sure I left Fez, the town where I was born, that very evening.

That happened many years ago. I look back on it today as one of the first signs of religious intolerance in Morocco. It was back in 1977!

Since then, I've continued to think deeply about Islam, studying it, reading texts and commentaries on it. I am moved and sometimes overwhelmed by the beauty of the Qur'an. But when I read the verses that speak of the punishments reserved for unbelievers, doubters and people who put their faith in more than one god, I can't help but be afraid.

If I know how to combat this fear, it's because my father showed me the way. He saw that Islam was not a constant presence in my life and that I did not practise my religion rigorously. 'You owe nothing to anyone on this Earth,' he said to me. 'You are responsible before God for your actions. If you do wrong, harm will come to you. If you do good, goodness will find you. What matters is that you are honourable, honest and fair, that you are true to your word, that you respect your parents and your teachers, that you are good, faithful and true. For the rest, you will see, God is great and merciful.'

Even so, over the last thirty years, Islam has come to represent a major problem in social and political life in France, and in Europe as a whole.

Living in a secular society, I have found the kind of freedom that does not exist in any Muslim country (not even in Turkey, as I explained to my daughter). The application of the principle of secularity is a mark of civilisation. The separation of church and state, of synagogue and state, of mosque and state is not in any way negative. On the contrary, it should be viewed as a mark of honour bestowed on religions.

But Islam does not sit well with the notion of secularity. Some Muslims adapt to it, while others simply do not comprehend the meaning of such a separation.

Freedom of expression is implicit in secularity. A freedom that has no limits. Whether we like it or are angered by it, we have to accept that those who express themselves in words, in poetry, in drawing and caricature have complete freedom to express their ideas and say what they think.

But it is so hard to get people to accept this idea: freedom of expression cannot be compromised. The millions of immigrant Muslims living and working in Europe are unable to accept blasphemy directed towards their Prophet. Christians or Jews pay no attention when blasphemy is directed towards their religions. But from the moment the Danish newspaper *Jyllands-Poste* gave ten or so of their cartoonists free rein to direct their talents at the Prophet of Islam in January 2005, the great majority of the Muslim population has been forced to understand what freedom of expression means in practice. And they see these cartoons as insults, as an attack on the dignity of a figure they consider to be sacred.

It would have been hard for a European to anticipate the reactions these cartoons were to provoke in the Muslim world: the violence and demonstrations, the inability to understand.

It was then that I realised how alone I was. I didn't see myself reflected in those hysterical mobs at all, and while I didn't approve of the publication of those cartoons, I did respect the authors' right to create them and make them publicly available. I thought they should have been treated with indifference.

That is the essence of what I wanted to convey to my daughter.

# ABOUT SMALL ✺ AXES

Founded in 2010 HopeRoad's mission has been to promote new literary voices from Africa, Asia and the Caribbean.

The name comes from a road in Jamaica where Bob Marley lived and which is now home to the Bob Marley Museum at 56 Hope Road.

In exploring themes of identity, cultural stereotyping and disability we bring neglected voices from the margins to the centre of the page in a range of books for adults and young adults.

Hard fought changes in attitudes are currently been reversed. We feel the need to launch a new imprint, Small Axes: inspired by the Bob Marley song, Small Axe: a well sharp axe ready to cut the big tree down. The imprint will mix post-colonial classics that helped to shape cultural shifts at the time of their first publication with titles by contemporary authors that continue in the tradition of rebellion and contesting the canon.

We hope that these books not only give pleasure, joy and entertainment, but that they also help to open minds and attitudes to diversity. We are pleased to be publishing in a period of cultural flux when more and more voices from outside the mainstream are being heard.

If you would like to support our work, please stay in touch online and via social media, details below.

Rosemarie Hudson, *Publisher and Founder of HopeRoad*
Pete Ayrton, *Editor Small Axes*

hoperoadpublishing.com | 🐦 📘 📷 @hoperoadpublish

# Other Small Axes Titles You Might Enjoy

hoperoadpublishing.com | 🐦 ❋ 📷 @hoperoadpublish

ARTEMISIA
Anna Banti
Translated by Shirley D'Ardia Caracciolo
Introduction by Susan Sontag

## COMING APRIL 2020

First published in 1953, *Artemisia* is a classic of 20th century Italian literature. From its first publication in 1953, *Artemisia*, a novel about Artemisia Gentileschi, an iconic 17th century painter, by Anna Banti, a brilliant Italian art historian, established itself as a feminist masterpiece. Artemisia is a book about the process of artistic creation. Much in Gentileschi's life marked her out as a victim – rape at the age of 18, a forced marriage to a man she did not love and, a powerful, patriarchal father, Orazio Gentileschi, who failed to value her artistic genius. But Gentileschi did not accept the status of victim, in the years between 1610 and 1650; she produced over 50 paintings that have established her as one of the great painters of all time. "What makes *Artemisia* a great book – and unique in Banti's work – is this double destiny, of a book lost and re-created. A book that by being posthumous, rewritten, resurrected, gained incalculably in emotional reach and moral authority. A metaphor for literature, perhaps. And a metaphor for reading, militant reading – which, at its worthiest, is rereading – too." Susan Sontag

ANNA BANTI, the pen name of Lucia Lopresti, was born in Florence in 1895. Like Artemisia Gentileschi, Anna Banti was always defined by a male mentor –in her case, her husband Roberto Longhi to whom *Artemisia* is dedicated. Until his death in 1970, Anna Banti lived in Roberto Longhi's shadow. Since then, like Artemisia, she has found an audience – inspired by feminism - able to appreciate her genius in its own right. The dialogue between author and subject in *Artemisia* is one of the great literary conversations of our time.

978-1-913109-00-4